Copyright © 2022 by Kyndall Bennett - All rights reserved.

The content contained within this book may not be reproduced, duplicated or transmitted without direct written permission from the author or the publisher.

Under no circumstances will any blame or legal responsibility be held against the publisher, or author, for any damages, reparation, or monetary loss due to the information contained within this book. Either directly or indirectly. You are responsible for your own choices, actions, and results.

Legal Notice:

This book is copyright protected. This book is only for personal use. You cannot amend, distribute, sell, use, quote or paraphrase any part, or the content within this book, without the consent of the author or publisher.

Disclaimer Notice:

Please note the information contained within this document is for educational and entertainment purposes only. All effort has been executed to present accurate, up to date, and reliable, complete information. No warranties of any kind are declared or implied. Readers acknowledge that the author is not engaging in the rendering of legal, financial, medical or professional advice. The content within this book has been derived from various sources. Please consult a licensed professional before attempting any techniques outlined in this book.

By reading this document, the reader agrees that under no circumstances is the author responsible for any losses, direct or indirect, which are incurred as a result of the use of the information contained within this document, including, but not limited to, — errors, omissions, or inaccuracies.

Additional Credit:

Cover design - Carolina Soares

Research - Publishing Services

Writing - Hanah Johnson

Editing - Aimee Jodoin

Visit the blog at KyrabeStories.com for more helpful resources.

She's Meant to Lead Available on Audible

Are you on a tight schedule? Scan the QR code below and download *She's Meant to Lead* from the Audible store to listen on the go!

Continue With the Series - She's Meant to Speak

With improved communication skills and confidence, you too can find your voice to speak against an unjust workplace and create a team bursting with healthy communication and diversity. Scan the QR code below to continue reading with book #2 in the series, *She's Meant to Speak*!

Contents

Introduction	1
1. Female Leaders Through History and Their Challenges	6
How Much Progression Has There Been?	
Why the Role of a Female Leader Is So Challenging	
2. Learning More About Yourself and Your Leadership Style	21
Twelve Common Leadership Styles	
What Is a Transformational Leader?	
What Is a Situational Leader?	
Discover Your Personal Leadership Style	
3. Overcoming Fear and Self-Doubt	47
Why Female Leadership Can Bring About Fear	
How to Overcome Anxiety and Fear of Leadership	
If You Doubt Your Skills, So Will Your Team	
4. Why Hard Skills Are Essential for Leaders	59
Seven Transferable Hard Skills	
5. Finding Your Voice and Making It Heard	69
The Gender Bias Lives On	
Understanding Effective Communication	
Getting Your Words Right	

      Completing the Communication Package
      Networking

6. Emotional Intelligence and Its Role in Leadership   84
      The Importance of Emotional Intelligence in the Workplace
      The Five Components of EQ
      How to Build Your Emotional Intelligence

7. Setting the Example for a Diverse Environment   93
      Why Is Diversity in the Workplace So Crucial?
      What Is Workplace Culture?
      Establishing a Growth Mindset Within Your Team
      Increasing Diversity in Your Team

8. Self-Care and the Imperative Balance   103
      The Silent Killer of the Workforce
      Self-Care for Leaders
      Self-Care for Your Professional Life
      Self-Care for Your Personal Life

Final Words   110

References   114

Acknowledgements   118

Introduction

"In the future, there will be no female leaders. There will just be leaders."
Sheryl Sandberg

Roughly half of the US workforce is made up of women. However, 35% of senior leadership positions are held by women, and of the Fortune 500 companies, only 8.2% of CEOs are women. Less than 1% of those positions are held by women of color (Ariella, 2022).

Throughout history, women have always held important positions in our communities. They were the doulas, the herbalists, the warriors, the gardeners, the mothers, the cooks, the managers, the animal breeders, the business owners, and more. Yet, despite our crucial importance in upholding our communities throughout history, we continue to be underrepresented in positions of power worldwide.

As women in business seeking professional development, our point of view is still hardly ever considered; it often seems as though our unique challenges as women are never taken seriously. We want to be great leaders in our workplaces, but female leadership stereotypes and expectations seem to hold us back unfairly. Even when supportive colleagues and bosses surround us, these stereotypes and expectations still cause fear and anxiety and act as a self-fulfilling prophecy, holding us back from becoming the great leaders we are destined to be.

In all honesty, we are still battling a world made for and by men. Whether in school, college, books written for leaders, or expectations at home or at work, many of us women have internalized leadership strategies that were designed with men in mind. While these strategies may work well for men, we find that they do not work for us because we are meant to lead in a different way. Quite frankly, our leadership capabilities give us an edge in the business world. If we only know how to tap into it.

Many of us are fed up with negative stereotypes about what it means to be a woman in the workforce. We suffer from inequality that often goes unnoticed or under the radar. Sometimes, we feel like incompetent leaders, blaming ourselves when things go wrong, even when we objectively did our best. Many of us lack the mental and emotional support systems we need to take on more responsibilities in the workplace. We don't want to fail and prove to people what we secretly fear: that we are not good enough leaders.

I have met many women who want to be leaders but can't shake the negative stereotypes associated with women who embody leadership qualities. We were mostly taught that good leaders are assertive and don't take no for an answer. Yet, at the same time, we've noticed that those women who do embody these qualities are often described as aggressive and even violent. We've been taught that a proper lady does not fit the idea of a genuine leader. We may want to leave these negative stereotypes behind us, but we still fear that people will judge us. We lack the confidence it takes to pursue leadership roles regardless of what people think or say. You may feel worried that others will judge you for putting effort into your professional life at the expense of your family, whether it's your children or elderly relatives.

Already, you can see that there are lots of stumbling blocks to becoming a woman leader in the business world. We have to work ten times hard for just a little bit of reward. We are held to much higher standards that simply cannot be reached. We have to contend with a gender wage gap that has no place in modern society, and we are attacked with stereotypes of women in leadership positions at every angle.

However, the good news is that women are gaining a foothold in leadership positions worldwide because of women like you who refuse to give up and want to speak up to have your voice heard in the business world. Although there are times when you may want to give up, you carry on marching bravely.

This book is for women like you and me, who continue to march on even when it's so tough we want to give up. I want to reassure you that there is a reward at the end of this process. Remember that those women who came before you had to go through this process to pave the path you walk through today. Because they made that sacrifice, you no longer have to be stuck in one position, afraid to move up, afraid to put yourself out there and chase your dreams. You no longer have to feel frustrated because you have not been making professional or personal progress, improving your community, your workplace, and your home.

As women, we have few examples of female leaders. While this lack of role models makes the goal of becoming leaders ourselves even harder to overcome, we can comfort ourselves with the knowledge that we continue to pave new pathways for the women who follow us, just as the women before us did.

As the Vice President of the United States, Kamala Harris, said: "I hope that by being a 'first,' I inspire young people to pursue their dreams. The number of times I've heard the word 'no'—or that something can't be done—in my lifetime is too many to count. I'm honored to be considered a 'first,' but I always think about the people who came before and paved the way for me to get where I am today. From Rosa Parks to Shirley Chisholm to Congressman John Lewis, I stand on the shoulders of so many great men and women before me."

Unlike men, we are underprivileged in the area of mentorship and role models. So, in this book, I want to fill in this mentorship gap by sharing with you fourteen leadership styles and techniques to create an empowering work environment: strategies that the women who came before us used to pave the road toward women's leadership.

If you are ready to make a difference for other women in your workplace, in your organization, in your community and in the world, then let's begin. It's not just about your leadership skills; it's about developing leadership skills and confidence among the women in your team, community, family, and friendship groups, and knowing that your leadership has a ripple effect can indeed change the world. Women make great leaders! And it's about time the world recognized us!

You may not have the skills to lead yet, but once you read this book, you will be able to face problems in your team caused by bad leadership, such as high turnover or toxic professional environments. You will learn how to tap into your personal leadership style to become a great leader. You will also learn strategies for overcoming your fear and self-doubt so that you can go after roles that are suited for you. Likewise, you will learn how to find your voice and effectively communicate so that you can make your voice heard in your workplace.

Women are often assumed to naturally have emotional intelligence, despite how sexist this assumption is. This book will imbue you with the emotional intelligence you need to be a great leader who sets examples for the diverse women and men in your team, your workplace, and your community.

Lastly, this book will encourage you to prioritize self-care so you can lead from a place of balance and self-love. By the end of this book, you will be confident and capable enough to lead your team and create a thriving work environment with a more diverse and inclusive workforce. This book is not just satisfied with teaching you how to be a great leader in your workplace and community; it is also concerned with teaching you how to leave your own positive mark on society, so society as a whole improves because of your actions.

Lastly, this book refrains from previous leadership tactics of assuming that only a particular group of people are interested in becoming good leaders. The desire to be a great woman leader cuts across race, ethnicity, nationality, sexuality, gender, religion, and age. As a result, you will find that this book also teaches you how to address biased beliefs that are still prominent in the professional world. The industries with the highest rates of women leaders today are HR, education/social services, healthcare, and hospitality, with law, medicine, and technology seeing a rise in popularity among women (Ariella, 2022). Whatever your industry, by the end of this book, you will have the skills you need to stand out as an individual, to excel in leadership, and to set an example for other team members regarding the future of leadership.

1
Female Leaders Through History and Their Challenges

"We may encounter many defeats, but we must not be defeated."
Maya Angelou

History has not been kind when recording women's achievements. Throughout the world, many women's achievements as leaders have been erased, forgotten, or rewritten so that, in some instances, men were given the glory. You may have encountered this situation in your workplace or in your personal relationships. You may already understand that this is not a new phenomenon. In this chapter, I will empower you by giving you examples of inspiring women from different fields throughout history and how they overcame the challenges they faced. We will also look at the challenges women face today and why there aren't more female leaders.

The good news is that history has still recorded some powerful women we can look to as role models. You might be wondering why we need to look back through history. After all, in recent decades, we have seen an explosion of women in power, as the above statistics show. Still, it's essential to know where you come from as a minority group. Knowing why you are fighting the good fight gives you a sense of empowerment.

As women, we need to be in leadership positions because we need strategic power. US Senator Elizabeth Warren says, "If you don't have a seat at the table, you're probably on the menu. Washington works for those who have power. And no one gives up power easily, no one ... Nobody's just going to say 'Women have arrived and let's just move over' ... We have a chance but we have to fight for it."

If you're on the menu, you're just an object with no agency. Those who have a seat at the table can make decisions about you that affect you without your input. Unfortunately, it is human nature for those in power to make decisions that benefit the powerful at the expense of minorities. This imbalance is what Elizabeth Warren is trying to warn us against. If we do not fight for a seat at the table, we will never be given one, and we will continue to be underrepresented. We will continue to live according to the decisions of those who do not understand our plight and struggles. For example, legislation that has been put into place worldwide to benefit women has come from women leaders who fully understand the female experience. As you will see from the examples provided in this chapter, those women we remember as leaders were able to change their lives and the lives of people around them by grabbing power and creating a seat at the table for themselves.

Make no mistake, we have a long way to go. According to the UN, "as of 19 September 2022, there are 28 countries where 30 women serve as Heads of State and/or Government. At the current rate, gender equality in the highest positions of power will not be reached for another 130 years" (UN Women, 2022). For the days you feel tired and need some encouragement to keep going, look back on this chapter to find examples of female leaders of the past who paved a way for us to make female leadership an accepted and expected goal for women today.

Queen Kubaba

In what is known as the first human civilization, Queen Kubaba became the first known female ruler in Sumeria, in the historical region of southern Mesopotamia. Known as one of the cradles of civilization, Sumeria was ruled by many kings. In 2400 B.C., however, Queen Kubaba bucked tradition and ascended the throne. In fact, Queen Kubaba was not only a queen, as she is studied to have been a successful business owner, brewing and selling beer!

Looking back at the history of powerful women, Egypt has many examples. The first recorded female ruler dates back to 4,500 years ago. In an article in Discover Magazine, writer Cody Cottier (2021) adds: "The story of powerful ancient women often centers on Egypt, where Sobekneferu, Hatshepsut, and Cleopatra reigned as pharaohs. But Kubaba ascended to the throne of Sumer long before them all, likely around 2400 B.C. To be clear, she was a true monarch—a queen regnant who ruled in her own right, rather than a queen consort, who is simply the wife of the monarch. The King List refers to her as lugal (king), not as eresh (queen consort). She is the only woman to bear this title."

At the same time, we must keep in mind that a leader is not defined only as someone who is running a country or even a business. A leader is also someone who shows up in their community and makes an impact. That being said, there have been influential women leaders throughout the world who have broken through some incredible challenges.

Sojourner Truth

Sojourner Truth, born Isabella Bomfree, was born into slavery in New York in 1797. As an enslaved person, she was bought and sold four times and received violent punishments from enslavers. She had to endure strenuous physical labor and eventually escaped in 1827 after an enslaver refused to free her in accordance with the New York Anti-Slavery Law of 1827, despite his promises. She would later say to him: "I did not run away, I walked away by daylight..."

In the 1830s, she became a charismatic speaker in New York City. By 1843, she renamed herself Sojourner Truth because she believed God had called her to preach the truth to the masses.

Truth was an abolitionist and gave many speeches about the evils of slavery. In 1850, she published her autobiography, *The Narrative of Sojourner Truth*. Although she could not read or write, she dictated this autobiography to writer Oliver Gilbert, who helped her publish the book.

Not only concerned with being an abolitionist, Truth was also a women's rights activist. You may have heard her most famous speech, and one of the most famous speeches in history, "Ain't I a Woman?" In the speech (National Park Service, 2022), she says:

> "That man over there says that women need to be helped into carriages, and lifted over ditches, and to have the best place everywhere. Nobody ever helps me into carriages, or over mud-puddles, or gives me any best place! And ain't I a woman? Look at me! Look at my arm! I have plowed and planted, and gathered into barns, and no man could head me! And ain't I a woman? I could work as much and eat as much as a man—when I could get it—and bear the lash as well! And ain't I a woman? I have borne thirteen children, and seen most all sold off to slavery, and when I cried out with my mother's grief, none but Jesus heard me! And ain't I a woman?

Then they talk about this thing in the head; what's this they call it? [member of audience whispers, "intellect"] That's it, honey. What's that got to do with women's rights or negroes' rights? If my cup won't hold but a pint, and yours holds a quart, wouldn't you be mean not to let me have my little half measure full?

Then that little man in black there, he says women can't have as much rights as men, 'cause Christ wasn't a woman! Where did your Christ come from? Where did your Christ come from? From God and a woman! Man had nothing to do with Him.

If the first woman God ever made was strong enough to turn the world upside down all alone, these women together ought to be able to turn it back, and get it right side up again! And now they is asking to do it, the men better let them."

Truth campaigned for the rights of Black women as she felt they were especially vulnerable in a white patriarchy in the United States. In fact, though she worked closely with famous abolitionist Frederick Douglass, Truth would later part with him because Douglass believed they should place the rights of Black women on the back burner and fight first for the rights of Black men. Likewise, Truth felt that the women's rights movement, championed by Susan B. Anthony and Elizabeth Cady Stanton, did not care about Black women, placing white women at the forefront over other women. Although Truth felt betrayed and dismissed by both Black male and white female leaders, she did not give up or give in. She refused to buy into the lie that white women and Black men deserved rights before Black women. Resolute, she stood firm in her belief that universal suffrage was the answer: everyone deserves equal rights simultaneously!

Truth was a human rights advocate, dedicating her life to helping enslaved people escape to freedom. When the Civil War began, she encouraged young men to join the Union to fight for the abolition of slavery. She organized supplies for Black troops during the war and, following the war, worked tirelessly to find jobs for freed slaves and help them to build their new lives. After the abolition of slavery, Truth lobbied tirelessly against segregation for the rest of her life. She was a warrior who believed she was called to be a voice for the oppressed in society. This empowering belief gave her the strength and courage to become a force of good for those around her.

Amelia Earhart

Amelia Earhart challenged conventions and changed how the world sees women. She was the first woman to attempt to fly around the world. She broke many records, like the women's altitude record of 14,000 feet. She was also the first woman to cross the Atlantic in a plane as a passenger. She caused a major storm when she broke this record, as she was seen as a breath of fresh air—a woman who played by her own rules and enjoyed life while doing so.

Even in her private life, Earhart never gave up her spirit of rebellion. She refused to change her name when she got married in 1931, believing that marriage was a partnership in which both partners were equal. She would later, in 1932, become the first woman to fly across the Atlantic solo, piloting her own plane. Unfortunately, in 1937, during her attempt to become the first woman to fly around the world, her plane was lost with just 7,000 miles remaining on her trip.

Amelia Earhart was never found, but her spirit of adventure, rebellion, and self-belief continues to inspire many women today.

Malala Yousafzai

Malala Yousafzai is the youngest person to ever receive the Nobel Peace Prize for her work. Born in Pakistan in 1997, Yousafzai's father was a champion of educational opportunities for girls. A teacher and an education advocate, he ran a girl's school in their village in Mingora. Yousafzai was one of his students. When she was ten years old, Taliban extremists began to prohibit many activities in the region. Girls were banned from attending school, playing music, and even owning a television.

In 2009, Yousafzai began blogging for the BBC under the pen name "Gul Makai." She wrote about her life as a young girl under Taliban rule and her desire to continue her education. As tensions rose in her region, she and her family moved away from their hometown. She and her father continued to advocate for Pakistani girls and their right to free education. Their work soon earned them international acclaim, and Yousafzai was soon nominated in 2011 for the International Children's Peace Prize. In the same year, she won Pakistan's National Youth Peace Prize.

Unfortunately, the following year, the Taliban accosted her while she was on a bus returning home from school with her friends. They shot her in the head and left her for dead. Malala was airlifted to a military hospital in Pakistan and then moved to an intensive care unit in England. Luckily, she didn't suffer any major brain damage, although she was left paralyzed on the left side of her face. After much surgery and rehabilitation, Yousafzai returned to normal life, this time in England.

Malala's dream is to keep fighting until every girl in the world is able to go to school. She published her autobiography, called *I Am Malala: The Girl Who Stood Up for Education and Was Shot by the Taliban*. This, coupled with her activism, won her the European Parliament's Sakharov Prize for Freedom of Thought. In 2014, she received the Nobel Peace Prize for activism for girls worldwide to receive a high-quality education. She continues to pursue her dreams, working hard to empower young women worldwide through innovative strategies and meeting with local advocates and leaders all over the globe.

These are but a few inspiring women—both past and present—who have inspired us to overcome the challenges we face in our lives. Their examples are a few out of the billions of challenges that women face daily. Personally, when I'm feeling down, when things don't go my way, and in those moments when I feel like giving up the fight, I like to read up on some of these great historical women to gain some necessary wisdom on how they overcame their challenges. Their determination and strength reignite my passion and gives me the courage I need to continue to push forward as a leader.

Here are some other women whose stories may give you that extra motivation to redefine what it means to be a leader and to create your own empowering work environment. You may already have your heroes who you look up to, not just for their perseverance in the face of adversity, but also for their tireless fight for their right to be leaders in their community.

- **Cleopatra VI** formed great political alliances and made Egypt into one of the world's greatest powers.

- **Joan of Arc** led the French army into battle victories and was later burned at the stake for challenging the patriarchy by being a great war leader. She would later be declared innocent.

- **Queen Victoria** revolutionized Great Britain during the Victorian era, bringing an entire country into modernity through her rulership.

- **Rosa Parks**, the "first lady of civil rights," changed the history of the United States of America by standing up for herself and refusing to give up her seat on the bus to a white man.

- **Margaret Thatcher**, the Iron Lady, wrangled her way into history books by overcoming high odds against serving as a female prime minister.

- **Angela Merkel**, one of the top European Union leaders before her retirement, saved the lives of millions of refugees by opening her country's borders and influenced the European Union in more ways than one.

- **Jane Austen** defined an entire literary genre and published some of the greatest novels in the English language, recognized the world over.

- **Maya Angelou** transformed from being a mute child into the civil rights activist, poet, and writer we remember today.

- **Marie Curie** faced constant discrimination as a woman in science despite her scientific advances that revolutionized the world.

- **Edith Cowan**, despite a troubled childhood, became a pioneer for women's rights and climbed her way to becoming the first Australian female member of parliament.

- **China Machado** redefined beauty by becoming the first model of color to pose in a major American fashion magazine (Harper's Bazaar) in 1959.

- **Tu Youyou**, a pharmaceutical chemist and malariologist, discovered one of the world's most effective anti-malarial drugs, artemisinin.

- **Serena Williams** is not only one of the world's greatest tennis players but one of history's most outstanding sportspersons.

How Much Progression Has There Been?

Considering we are looking at 4,500 years since the first female leader, progress has been slow. We've already seen in this chapter that there is a massive gap between genders when it comes to political leadership. Still, we've also noticed that these gaps are closing. In 2021, women in senior roles increased by 31%, the biggest increase in history. Worldwide, 90% of companies had at least one woman in a senior management role. Further good news is that, though they are still more likely to be in HR, there is a growing number of female CEOs and managing directors: 26% in 2021 compared with 15% in 2019. In 2021, there were twenty-three female CEOs in the Fortune Global 500, six of whom were women of color (Catalyst, 2021).

Aside from the challenges, one of the biggest problems concerning women in leadership is the difference in pay. In 2020, 53.1% of PhDs in the US were earned by women. Yet, women who earned a Master's degree earned an average salary of $72,568, while men with the same level of education earned an average of $117,617.

Just a century ago, we would not even have had any of these statistics. Yet today, we continue to push back against a system designed for men, demanding our right to be leaders, bosses, and influential people. In retrospect, we have fought hard to get where we are. This alone is deserving of recognition and praise. We have gone from having our feet bound, being sold as slaves and child brides, to becoming the greatest sportspeople in history, brilliant scientists making innovative discoveries, and champions for the rights and education of women and girls worldwide. I believe that women's achievements in the past century are not celebrated as much as they should be. That is why it is crucial to remind yourself when you feel low and want to give up that we have excelled beyond society's limitations.

We have progressed so far and so well; there is just no reason for you to stop now!

Why the Role of a Female Leader Is So Challenging

Being a leader, regardless of gender, is difficult. It requires a multitude of skills and the discernment to know when to use those skills, what to do in specific and difficult situations, and how to handle crises without letting them get to you in the moment. It is not a job for the faint-hearted.

Before even getting into the role of leadership, women already face additional challenges in the workforce. These include:

Insufficient Childcare/Caregiver Support

Women still carry the brunt of the responsibility of childcare around the world. Childcare is still seen predominantly as a "woman's job," and women are expected to give up their professional working lives to look after their children full-time. It is still seen as taboo for men to take on childcare responsibilities, so women often find themselves with not just significant gaps in their CV, but also gaps in their knowledge and expertise as their industry leaves them behind during those years when they take time off to focus on their children.

Likewise, women have reported that they received more promotions and bigger work responsibilities, once they passed "childbearing age." This led them to believe that companies were hesitant to give them more significant responsibilities at work in their "childbearing years" because of a fear that they would have to take maternity leave. While this is illegal, it still occurs frequently.

Lack of Access to Remote or Flexible Work

Women with families tend to work better with remote or flexible work because they have more time to dedicate to their families, as well as their work. For women who may not have families to take care of, remote/flexible work gives them additional time to study and improve their qualifications.

In recent years, some women have argued that menstrual cycles also need to be accounted for in our workplaces. For many women, the reality is that they need to continue to go into work even on those days when they are suffering severe symptoms of PMS.

The Gender Pay Gap

Despite women's efforts to close the gender gap, this dream still leaves a lot to be done. Due to the COVID-19 pandemic, many women lost positions at work or found themselves becoming stay-at-home caregivers to take care of their families (WE Forum, 2020). This has only served to increase the gender wage gap. Other factors continue to feed the gender pay gap as we know it today. According to the Harvard Business Review (Bolotnyy and Emmanuel, 2022):

> "Despite substantial progress toward pay equity, women in 2022 still earn 17% less than men on average. Many explanations for this gap have been proposed: Women may choose to work in lower-paying occupations; they may have less experience due to having taken time off to have kids or care for elders; they may shy away from negotiation or competition; they may be passed over by managers, perhaps due to conscious or unconscious bias."

Lack of Sponsorship

Nepotism and unconscious bias are still very much alive in the professional world. Unfortunately for women, this often means that men receive most of the sponsorship opportunities in the workplace and within academics. Women are considered risk investments, whereas men benefit from an unconscious bias that deems them a safe bet. This self-fulfilling prophecy, therefore, benefits men over women.

Unconscious Bias

The Unconscious Bias Project (2022) defines unconscious bias as:

> "Prejudice in favor of or against one thing, person, or group compared with another, usually in a way considered to be unfair. Unconscious bias can manifest in many ways, such as how we judge and evaluate others, or how we act toward members of different groups.

> The primary literature shows people can harbor unconscious biases against, for example, white women or people of color, even when that

person consciously believes that sexism and racism are wrong."

From this definition alone, we can all agree that we've all faced unconscious bias. Women, in particular, have an almost unlimited amount of unconscious stereotypes that people apply to them. We are continually placed inside restrictive boxes and punished when we naturally move out of these boxes. After all, we are all unique individuals and cannot be defined as simple stereotypes! There is always more to every one of us.

Still, people refuse to acknowledge our differences and uniqueness when we step out of these boxes that society forces us in. We've all heard people say, for example, "Oh, you'll change your mind once you meet the right man" when a woman says she doesn't want to have children. Or "It must be that time of the month" when a woman reacts angrily to someone crossing her boundaries.

Unconscious bias is far more insidious than it sounds. For example, some women cry when they are angry or frustrated. Since our workforce is built around ideals of masculinity (stoicism), emotional reactions, such as crying, are automatically interpreted as a weakness (a lack of stoicism). Therefore, a woman who cries at her coworker's frustrating and disrespectful behavior may not be promoted by her boss because her boss thinks she is weak, "too emotional," and therefore unable to handle a leadership position. Unconscious bias prevents us from truly understanding people who look different from us on the outside. As a result, women are often misjudged and prejudged and deemed unsuitable for leadership positions based on sexist, limited, and ignorant unconscious biases.

Women in leadership may have to face these issues and be held to higher standards, fight more gender stereotypes, play the same workplace strategies created for men, manage multiple roles, and take risks in a world with no safety net.

Life certainly can be more challenging for female leaders, but it doesn't mean that female leadership is impossible, and it doesn't mean that it isn't worth it!

Chapter Summary

- Women need to be in leadership positions because we are underrepresented in positions of power.

- To gain strategic power, we must grab a seat at the table. We cannot wait for men to give us power, as this will never happen.

- Although we've made unbelievable progress in the past century, we have a long way to go.

- Do your research on some of history's great historical women to gain some necessary wisdom on how they overcame their challenges.

- Women face additional challenges in the workforce, including lack of sponsorship, unconscious bias, a widening gender pay gap, lack of access to remote or flexible work, and insufficient childcare/caregiver support.

In the next chapter, you will learn how to find a leadership style that works for you and increases your confidence. The first stage to successful leadership, regardless of gender, is understanding the different styles. The goal is not to force yourself into a specific leadership style but to use your understanding of all the styles to adopt or develop your own preferences. This is how you become a natural leader and bring about gender equality in your workplace!

2
Learning More About Yourself and Your Leadership Style

"We need to reshape our own perception of how we view ourselves. We have to step up as women and take the lead."
Beyonce Knowles

Bossy, aggressive, pushy, angry, hysterical, cold, calculating, ballbusters, careerist... These are all adjectives that are too often used to describe female leaders. On the other hand, men are often labeled as decisive, strong, assertive, authoritative, and intelligent when they exhibit the same leadership qualities. Bear in mind that it is not only men who have been known to use these negative adjectives as insults against women. Even women have been caught using them on their peers.

In the last chapter, I gave an example of a woman who cries when she feels frustrated or angry. A man, on the other hand, is more likely to shout or punch a wall when he feels angry. He may decide to stonewall whoever made him mad in the workplace, causing a breakdown in communication. Nevertheless, we all know that the woman is more likely to be punished, judged, and perceived negatively for reacting out of anger than the man would. It's accepted that a male leader can lose his rag, but women aren't afforded the same luxury, much less women of color. You can imagine what people say about a Black woman who displays her anger in the workplace. Black women already suffer from the stereotype of the "angry Black woman," so any reactions from her will be considered, unjustly, as coming from a place of her "innate" angry state. These double standards are incredibly unfair toward us.

To overcome this, it is worth investigating different leadership styles, taking the best qualities out of each one to create your own unique style that is far removed from the stereotypes that women have to deal with.

One of the biggest mistakes we can make is to copy the leadership styles of men. This is not because men's leadership styles are wrong but because we are trying to be someone we aren't. We will never truly achieve the success that belongs to us when we try to be someone we are not. Sonya Sotomayor, US Supreme Court Justice, said poignantly:

> "I have a style that is Sonia, and it is more assertive than many women are, or even some men. And it's a style that has held me generally in good stead. There's nothing wrong with being a little bit quieter than me or more timid than me, but if you're doing it all of the time and not waiting for the moments where you need to be more assertive and take greater control, then you won't be successful. And I don't think I would have been successful if I didn't know how to soften myself and tone it down at important moments."

Likewise, Jacinda Ardern, Prime Minister of New Zealand, said:

> "One of the criticisms I've faced over the years is that I'm not aggressive enough or assertive

enough, or maybe somehow, because I'm empathetic, it means I'm weak. I totally rebel against that. I refuse to believe that you cannot be both compassionate and strong."

Today, Prime Minister Ardern is one of the most influential leaders in the world, admired for her country's empathetic response to the COVID-19 pandemic. We can learn from both Ardern and Sotomayor that it is essential to find a style that works for your unique blend of personalities. So, without further ado, let's take a look at typical leadership styles and how you can use these to find a kind that makes you a confident leader.

Twelve Common Leadership Styles

The most effective leaders are self-aware. This means they know their strengths, weaknesses, and styles and adopt them to meet different scenarios. Here are the twelve most common leadership styles:

The Affiliative

The affiliative leader creates an emotional bond with their team, putting people before profit. Affiliative leaders believe that the best way to run a workplace is by focusing on team building, positivity building, and creating a harmonious workplace (Indeed, 2020). It's all about the inner workings of the team with an affiliative leader. This leader employs conflict resolution and problem-solving to meet the team's emotional needs and foster harmony in the workplace.

Naturally, affiliative leadership promotes happy workplaces. Team members feel more connected and feel that their emotional and social needs are met. One important aspect of affiliative leadership is motivating your employees by using rewards and emotional validation. Affiliative leaders are also more likely to bend the rules and create flexible work conditions that make employees happy.

Ironically, because the affiliative leader is focused on creating positivity and harmony, employees may feel less willing to give negative feedback, either because they do not want to seem ungrateful or because they believe that the workplace must always be positive. If some of your team members are not motivated by rewards and emotional validation, they may not work as hard.

The Authoritarian

The authoritarian makes decisions without input from their team. The authoritarian believes that only they should hold all the power in the workplace. This leadership style is similar to dictatorships and is often seen used in the military, gangs, and the mafia (Brinn, 2014).

As you can imagine, this leadership style comes in handy when an important decision needs to be made on the spot. An authoritarian with a lot of knowledge, intelligence, and creativity will be able to make quick decisions that benefit those working for them. On the other hand, a wise leader understands that no one can do it alone: nobody knows everything. This is why world leaders have advisors and ministers. Consequently, an authoritarian leader will inevitably make serious mistakes that affect their entire team. In fact, if you research dictatorships in history, you'll find that they all ended up as failed states because of the dictator's hubris.

In authoritarian-dominated workplaces, those working for the leader are not permitted or encouraged to voice their opinions. This can easily lead to creating a workplace ruled by fear and anxiety. Your team will not be as productive as they should in such an environment.

Authoritarian leadership is destined to fail if used irresponsibly, inappropriately, and insensitively. It sends a message to your team that you are arrogant and too insecure to consider the viewpoints of others. However, you can still choose to be assertive, making the last call on important decisions after listening to what your team has to say, and allowing your team members to also make decisions when possible.

The Bureaucratic

The bureaucratic leader is similar to the authoritarian leader in that they both love the chain of command. Both types of leaders believe that it is the job of the employees to follow. Whereas the authoritarian leader believes that the employee must follow only them, the bureaucratic leader believes that the employee must follow regulations without fail. The bureaucratic leader also believes there is a clear stratification of authority in the workplace and everyone must follow it.

The bureaucratic leader differs from the affiliative leader, who will bend the rules to ensure a harmonious workplace. On the other hand, the bureaucratic leader would rather get rid of employees than bend rules. These strategies can be experienced heavily in industries that require less individual creativity but substantial emphasis on safety procedures and regulations, such as frontline manufacturing positions or roles that require higher security clearances where protective regulations are significantly less compromising.

Note that this strict environment can create an atmosphere of fear. Such a rigid leadership style does not promote a productive workplace, especially where creativity and innovation are needed to thrive. There will always come times when you have to do things outside the set restrictions and regulations;

however, the strictest bureaucratic leaders will refuse to acknowledge this. This ultimately leads to unproductive, unhappy, and unmotivated workers.

Bureaucratic leaders can also be considered insecure because their employees perceive them to be fearful of taking risks and making their own independent decisions. While a bureaucratic leader can find solutions by the book, they are still left unable to find solutions outside the box—a big weakness in their leadership style. This lack of creativity and independent thinking also means their employees may not respect them. Similarly, because this leadership style is so focused on regulations and rules, the leader misses the fact that each member of the team is a unique individual. This leads to depersonalization, leaving individuals feeling looked over and invalidated.

The Coach

The coach invests energy and time in boosting the team's strengths. Like the affiliative leader, the coach is interested in the inner workings of their employees. The coach recognizes that their employees work better through motivation. However, unlike the affiliative leader, the coach is able to use different methods for motivating their employees. This means that the coach does not necessarily have to take a method where they promote a harmonious workplace. A coach can also take a more authoritarian method when coaching their employees. You see this often in the sports world, where coaches of different teams are known for having different coaching approaches. In that sense, the coaching approach toward leadership is much more flexible because it gives the leader different strategies for coaching and, ultimately, leading the team.

A healthy coach needs to achieve the right balance between praise and criticism. A coach that can give criticism with compassion and emotional intelligence is able to lead their team efficiently. On the other end of the spectrum, a coach who cannot provide their employees criticism with compassion and empathy will destroy their enthusiasm for their work, decreasing work efficiency and output in the workplace.

If done correctly, the coaching approach toward leadership achieves a great balance between meeting individual workers' needs and the team's needs. Conversely, without emotional intelligence, a coach cannot achieve this balance, leaving the team and individuals within the team feeling frustrated, overlooked, and unmotivated.

Coaching also involves regularly taking time away from bureaucratic and organizational practices in the workplace to dedicate time toward staff coaching and development. This may seem like a disadvantage in the short-term, but the time "lost"when coaching is gained in improved quality of work. Coaching your employees at first may take more energy and time, but you will see results over time. Employees who are regularly coached feel appreciated. An appreciated employee is a happy one, and a happy employee produces better quality of work. The coaching method of leadership may be more difficult to implement if you work in a high-pressure workplace where results need to be immediate. In high-paced workplace environments, coaching might end up taking a backseat.

Lastly, an effective coach must have the emotional intelligence to understand the personalities and character of each of their employees. That way, the leader's coaching can be tailored to each employee's personality: to meet each employee's needs.

The Democratic

Democratic leadership is also known as participative leadership. It is simply based on the idea of democracy: everyone has a say in workplace decisions. The democratic leader encourages employees to exchange their ideas freely. Just like in a democratic government, discussion is actively encouraged. This type of leader believes in the ideals of liberty, equality, and fraternity—the three principles behind the French Revolution that would eventually birth democracy itself. This is not to say that the democratic leader does not still have the final say in decision-making processes; however, the democratic leader considers everyone's viewpoints and will allow employees to vote on workplace matters when beneficial.

The democratic leader wants to hear everyone's voice. As a result, the democratic leader values diversity because diverse people offer new points of view and varied skills and knowledge that improve efficiency, quality, and output in the workplace. Naturally, employees in this workplace feel prompted to rely on their creativity to find solutions. Hence, creative thinkers thrive under democratic leadership.

Conversely, employees who prefer a more bureaucratic workplace environment may struggle to adapt to a democratic leadership that prioritizes creativity when solving problems. Democratic leaders also need to find ways to include timid or unresponsive employees who may not want to voice their opinions for different reasons—for example, a fear that they may face retaliation for giving a dissenting opinion. A reliable democratic leader will see this challenge as a chance to improve their own leadership and people management skills.

You can incorporate other types of leadership into a democratic leadership. A democratic leadership can be bureaucratic, for instance. They could also be a coach. This is a great advantage to democratic leadership, as it allows for great versatility and creativity. Note that a democratic leader will still lead based on their morals and values. This can cause friction between you and employees who disagree with your morals and values. This friction is quite common in democracies where dissenting voices often cannot come to a compromise. A diligent democratic leader will always seek a compromise that makes everyone feel validated and respected.

Still, having a diverse group of employees does not automatically mean they have great decision-making skills. It is possible to have employees with poor skills and a lack of understanding of the present issues. A democratic leader must be able to gauge whether or not they can trust the decision-making skills of their employees. Likewise, for a democratic leadership style to work, the leader must watch out for communication failures. For example, since so many employees may give their input on workplace matters, there is bound to be miscommunication. Therefore, the democratic leader must find ways to prevent communication failures.

The Emergent

Emergent leadership differs from the other leadership styles because emergent leaders are not elected or hired. Rather, they emerge organically. The emergent leaders happen to be at the right place at the right time, like in a moment of crisis, where they take the necessary action to avert disaster. Emergent leaders display leadership traits at the exact moment a leader is needed. This is usually not done deliberately, as emergent leaders are usually not interested in climbing the corporate ladder—especially through traditional ways.

You can say that emergent leaders gained the role through a natural route, as they displayed their leadership qualities organically. Emergent leaders are usually well-respected and supported by both their employers and their employees. Why? Being able to display leadership qualities at the exact moment it is needed suggests that a person naturally has these traits and has taken the time and effort needed to develop said traits. After all, leadership is a skill that requires constant development. In essence, an emergent leader is a disciplined individual, not because they want to climb the corporate ladder but because they believe in discipline as a personal value. Disciplined people are usually well-respected; since they are well-respected, emergent leaders naturally make good leaders. Simply put, we all like to follow leaders we respect.

This respect from employees gives emergent leaders the support and recognition they need to improve their confidence in their performance and decision-making skills. Consequently, they make good choices, increasing their employees' respect for them, and promoting a happy workplace for everyone involved.

Typically, emergent leaders are accepted by their employees because they fit in well with the workplace dynamic. Nevertheless, emergent leaders may lose their employees' support and recognition if they do not meet the expectations put on them by the group members. Unfortunately, emergent leaders feel this pressure between meeting the expectations of the employees (who are their former group members) and also leading appropriately. As such, an emergent leader has to have a solid identity to make unpopular decisions for the group that promoted them to leaders in the first place. An efficient emergent leader has to be adaptable, moving fluidly between the expectations of the group and of their employers.

The Laissez-Faire

The laissez-faire leader has a live-and-let-live attitude. This leader prefers to hand out tasks to their employees and simply leave them to the responsibilities.

This leader is the complete opposite of the micromanager. Whereas a micromanager may ask for updates on a project every day, the laissez-faire leader may not even ask for updates. They expect the work to be completed by the deadline. Some laissez-faire leaders may even grant you extra time without much pushback.

The laissez-faire leader is often well-liked. Their employees don't feel stressed out or disrespected by micromanaging tactics. Most often, employees feel respected by a laissez-faire attitude because this leader inadvertently reveals, through their actions, that they trust their employees. Employees who feel respected by their leaders often work hard, not wanting to disappoint their employer. Most of us have had our share of bad leaders, so when we meet a leader that makes us feel respected, we work hard to keep working for them. We don't want to work under another bad leader after enjoying the experience of working for a leader who makes us feel that they respect our humanity and dignity.

This is all well and good when you have employees who are responsible and willing to do the work. However, a laissez-faire attitude does not work with certain employees, namely employees who might be lazy or who work better when they are under stress. Once an employee begins to miss deadlines repeatedly, a laissez-faire attitude will not work, and you will need to interfere. As a laissez-faire leader, you must ensure that your live-and-let-live attitude comes from respect for the employees rather than a desire to be liked or fear of angering or upsetting employees. A laissez-faire leader who cannot be strict when the situation calls for it will be inefficient.

Additionally, sometimes laissez-faire leadership comes from a place of laziness on the part of the leader. A laissez-faire leader who expects their employees to make all the decisions in the workplace will soon find themselves losing the respect of their employees. To be effective, laissez-faire leadership must also be accompanied by responsibility and hard work on the leader's part and be partnered with a more authoritative leadership style when needed.

The Pacesetter

The pacesetter is the leader we all need but may not necessarily like. We appreciate the fact that they push us to get results, but we also are not fond of the fact that they push us to get results.

The pacesetter has high standards for themselves, which they expect others to follow. They believe that results have a good metric for determining whether the workplace is efficient and effective. Therefore, employees working under a pacesetter leader are expected to produce results. Pacesetter leaders can be quite effective but can also be detrimental to the employees' mental and emotional health. It all depends on how they prefer to get results.

As with all leadership styles, the pacesetter leads first from who they are. A pacesetter leader who pushes themselves too hard from a place of insecurity and overcompensation will also expect their employees to do the same. This may work for other employees who also prefer to work very hard; however, this will only produce short-term results in employees who prefer a moderate pace at work. Eventually, employees will burn out and begin to produce bad work or leave. Even worse, employees may begin to make mistakes and have accidents that could be seriously detrimental to the workplace and the organization.

Concurrently, a pacesetter who pushes themselves from an understanding that they can do better and be better will be able to achieve results on a long-term basis and without detriment to their employees' and organizations' health. Pacesetters are often Type A personalities. They love to get results. A healthy pacesetter can tell when to take breaks, when to pull back, when to take a laissez-faire approach to leadership, and when to step in. While some of the greatest leaders in history have been emergent leaders—for example, Malala Yousafzai—others have been pacesetters who also knew they could be more in life. They understood they could only achieve more by pushing harder than was expected by those around them. A great example of a pacesetter is Amelia Earhart.

Pacesetters must be compassionate to understand that people ultimately come before goals and results. At the same time, they must also have the drive and conviction to convince their employees to push themselves further. An inspirational pacesetter is a self-regulating one. Similarly, pacesetting leadership does not work well with certain types of leadership that prioritize strict organizational work. Pacesetters are known for breaking the rules, while you cannot break the rules under bureaucratic leadership.

The Servant

The servant leader believes that a genuine leader serves. This leader believes that, by serving the needs of their employees, they can enrich the lives of their workers and, ultimately, build a better organization—and even a better world.

The servant is similar to the affiliative because they both believe in caring for people. They love to create emotional bonds with employees, believing that this bond is what drives profit and success for their organization. One key difference between both parties is that the servant leader may not necessarily be as in tune with the emotional needs of their employees as the affiliative may be.

A less emotionally healthy servant may believe that they can serve their employees by being bureaucratic and meeting their workplace's organizational needs—for example, by ensuring that there are enough office supplies and that office equipment is working efficiently at all times. A more emotionally intelligent servant will attempt to build a workplace culture where employees feel valued. They achieve this by ensuring that employees feel heard and validated. They attempt to build a community where employees feel cared for.

Nevertheless, both the affiliative and the servant will employ conflict resolution and problem-solving skills when needed to ensure that the needs of their employees are met. Both the servant and the affiliative believe that happy employees who feel emotionally and organizationally fulfilled make a workplace successful.

While employees may not feel confident or willing to give negative feedback to the affiliative leader, they may feel more confident giving negative feedback to the servant. Why? The servant may not be as concerned with creating a positive emotional environment as the affiliative. They are not just servants to their employees but also to their organization and clients/customers. As a result, they also like to focus on business success metrics, such as client satisfaction, organizational aims, business strategy, and financial goals.

The servant leader's preoccupation with serving can be an advantage because servant leaders believe it's their job to provide their employees with all the facilities they need for development. They won't hesitate to invest in their employees, providing them with development opportunities to improve their skills. This is a long-term strategy that servants use to enable business success.

With a servant mindset, leaders are not afraid to take risks. Servants are often in touch with who they are. It takes humility to believe that your role as a leader is to serve others. To reach this level of humility, an individual needs to be emotionally intelligent. They need the confidence to take risks to meet organizational goals. This risk-taking ability gives employees confidence in the servant's decision-making skills and ability to absorb any mistakes' negative consequences.

Alternatively, a servant who believes they should serve the needs of the shareholders and the organization's bottom line will feel as though they should prioritize these above their employees' happiness, satisfaction, and care. If the organization is interested in financial and business results above all, the servant will prioritize this as well.

The Strategic

The strategic leader is an interesting mix between the pacesetter, the bureaucratic, and their own personal leadership style. Strategic leaders, as the name suggests, are all about strategy. They are all about what works best. They employ efficiency at all levels of business. Nonetheless, strategic leaders are only bureaucratic when it makes sense. They are also quite open-minded and willing to try new ways of doing things as long as they bring about results.

This open-mindedness and flexibility, along with organizational and bureaucratic skills, allow strategic leaders to evolve, albeit within the confines of their organization's vision. Strategic leadership is a long-term leadership style; evaluating it from a short-term perspective makes it seem chaotic. If you look at the long-term results of this leadership style, many will find it cleverly successful. Strategic leaders use patterns to determine which business strategies are most likely to be successful and which are most likely to fail—and for what reason.

Strategic leadership is an essential tool for organizations that want to be successful. Without strategy, organization, and the flexibility and open-mindedness to go with the flow, an organization will surely fail.

Unfortunately, a strategic leader's main strength is also their main weakness. It may be a gamble whether a particular strategy is going to be successful in the long-term. Organizations are not set in stone. There are always internal and external factors pushing and pulling an organization in different directions, such as the economy, government policies, current events, and so on. This can all affect a leader's strategy. Suppose an organization and a leader have invested plenty of resources in following a particular strategy. In that case, they could face a big blow from changing too many factors, possibly leaving the strategy less effective or useless. No one can predict things like the global economy, political instability, and worldwide epidemics.

Strategic leadership also requires significant expense. A reliable strategic leader will learn to be flexible, so they can make changes and modifications to their strategy without losing sight of their goals—and without incurring too many expenses.

Great strategic leaders are visionaries who are able to see long-term results that others cannot see. On the other hand, sometimes this can mean that the strategist forgets short-term organizational goals in favor of the bigger picture. Naturally, this can lead to pressing problems that only serve to undermine the organization's goals. Therefore, strategic leaders must ensure they give as much attention to the organization's short-term goals as they do to the long-term objectives. A strategic leader must also remember that they may be able to see long-term goals clearly, but their employees may not. This means that strategic leaders must co-adopt a coaching leadership style that will enable them to help their employees envision the bigger picture.

In many cases, organizations have to work tirelessly for months or years before they see success under strategic leadership. This sudden success can be overwhelming for employees who are not used to working under a strategic leadership style. Again, employees in this scenario will need coaching from the strategic leader to help them process the sudden changes in their organization.

The Transactional
Transactional leadership is also known as managerial leadership. It is a leadership style that believes that employees should be both rewarded and punished as a way to motivate success in the workplace. The transactional leader uses tactics

such as group performance, supervising employees closely, and setting specific goals.

Transactional leadership is similar to bureaucratic leadership because both styles of leadership focus on rigid structures within the workplace. This ideology is where the similarity ends, however, because the transactional leader believes that structure and organization in the workplace is a means to an end. The bureaucratic leader believes that following set organizational structures is the only way to run a business. Alternatively, the transactional leader believes that employees should follow their leadership alone, rather than follow bureaucracy in itself. The bureaucratic leader could be also a laissez-faire leader as long as their employees follow organizational structures and procedures; the transactional leader, by virtue of the leadership style, cannot be laissez-faire. This leader believes that their employees must be monitored carefully to ensure they are working at or above expectations.

Transactional leadership uses human psychology and behavior rather than organizational bureaucracy. It follows the ideology that humans work better when they are rewarded for success and fear repercussions for failure. In a transactional workplace, employees are expected to conform to rules and regulations, and they will be punished if their performance does not meet expectations. At the same time, the transactional leader uses rewards as bait, trying to lure employees into chasing the prizes promised to them when they succeed.

Already, you may be able to spot the flaw in this sort of leadership style. What happens if an employee follows the rules and regulations exactly but still fails, for example, because the rules and regulations do not empower the employee to succeed? Under transactional leadership, employees are often punished, despite following procedures. It is easy for a transactional leader to blame their employees for not meeting expectations without examining whether their employees have been given the right tools. Certainly, transactional leadership works when employees are given the resources needed to meet expectations.

Nonetheless, this sort of leadership style promotes an atmosphere of anxiety and fear within the workplace. Some people can thrive in such an environment; others find it stifling, causing their work productivity, success, and efficacy to plunge.

Transactional leaders are not the visionaries that strategic leaders are. They want tangible, quantitative results in the short term. They want to promote and reinforce the status quo of the workplace. If the workplace has high employee productivity and financial success levels, then maintaining this status quo is a great goal. On the other hand, if the organization needs change before it can find success, then maintaining the status quo will lead to the inevitable: organizational failure. Likewise, a successful organization still has to deal with changing external factors. Organizations must review their structures and objectives to meet an ever-changing world. During times of change, transactional leaders can be a liability because they are better suited to keeping the status quo, not changing it using visionary leadership. Transactional leaders who can use their leadership style to bring about positive change are better suited to a changing organization.

If transactional leaders are able to incorporate other forms of leadership styles, such as the affiliative style, into their own leadership, then they will be able to create a workplace that is kind, caring, and compassionate toward employees. Conversely, a transactional leader who employs less emotional and more structural leadership styles (such as bureaucratic leadership and strategic leadership) into their personal style may find their employees feel invalidated and disvalued. This could lead to high turnover, employee dissatisfaction, and less success for the organization.

The Visionary

The visionary and the strategic leader both share one unique characteristic: both envision a future that others may not necessarily be able to see. The strategic leader tends to see a future that is based on facts around them. That means that they plan their goals based on the reality they observe. This helps them determine whether a particular strategy will be successful in the long term. The visionary may also operate in this way. One certain thing is that the visionary has an idea of how their workplace should exist. They are idealists. Unlike the strategist, the visionary wants to create a whole new world that has never been seen before.

The visionary is a dreamer who makes their dreams come true. They dream of potential change in the workplace and, moreover, are able to lead the employees to create this new vision. Compare that to the transactional leader who can lead their team to achieve goals but may not necessarily believe in the vision that created those goals. The visionary combines the best of both worlds: dreaming dreams and achieving results.

The visionary is a risk-taker. Like the strategic leader, the visionary understands that their goals are long-term goals. As a result, the visionary is content to make sacrifices and commit to achieving these goals. You cannot have change without risk or change. This can be concerning for employees who prefer safety in the workplace. These employees may see the visionary as someone with wild, crazy ideas that may never be fulfilled. Visionaries work best when surrounded by employees who believe in their vision and are willing to commit to it.

Successful visionary leaders usually like their employees to be honest with them about their ideas and their goals. Consequently, a successful visionary leader will surround themselves not only with like-minded visionary employees but also employees who think and see the world differently from them. These leaders need more bureaucratic and tempered employees to bring an element of realism to their dream. The visionary needs employees who understand how the status quo works and how to manipulate the status quo to bring forth change.

An influential visionary leader must be willing to listen to their employees and be willing to take negative criticism without getting defensive. This negative criticism is important for helping the visionary build borders to contain their dream from over-expanding and becoming uncontrollable. It is also important for the visionary leader to bear most, if not all, of the risk of chasing their dream. They recognize that it is not fair to allow their employees to bear the brunt of any negative consequences of their own risk. Hence, this leader will try their best to shoulder the risk, ensuring that their employee is protected. Despite the best efforts of the visionary, their employees may still have to take on the negative consequences that come with this risk.

The visionary leader also runs into the same problem as the strategic leader: they cannot accurately measure whether their long-term strategy/plan will see success. As with all risks, visionary leadership has the propensity that can go very wrong, but it also has the reward of incredible success, should it go right.

Personality-wise, visionary leaders tend to be thinkers. Thinkers tend to have positive ethics and values. Consequently, the visionary's employees often feel cared for and respected. These leaders love to set expectations by example rather than through reward and punishment. This means that those employees who naturally cannot meet these expectations filter themselves out. No doubt, employees of the visionary grow exponentially in their role, both personally and professionally, because they are constantly challenged at the workplace.

What Is a Transformational Leader?

As well as the twelve leadership styles, there is also the transformational leader. They are concerned about the advancement of others, and they inspire people to meet expectations and work toward a common goal. This is done based on four components: intellectual stimulation, individualized consideration, inspirational motivation, and idealized influence. Research shows that these leaders create higher levels of performance and satisfaction. Transformational leadership can also have a positive impact on employee well-being.

For women, this style can be especially beneficial. Think of the stereotype of the visionary leader, for example. Most of the visionary leaders we've celebrated in the last few centuries have been men. Women visionary leaders like Hillary Clinton face constant ridicule from society for daring to dream of a different world. It can be difficult for women to choose a leadership style that defers stereotypes and encourages disdain from their local community and society at large. This is why transformational leadership works well for women since it allows women to be leaders and still avoid the emotional abuse that women leaders are prone to experience. Additionally, the traits of a transformational leader fit into the expectations of feminine traits, including open-mindedness, active listening skills, supportiveness, emotional intelligence, encouraging others to communicate, engineering unity and peace between people, and problem-solving skills. Transformational leaders use interpersonal skills to boost their employees' morale, motivate them, and improve their job performance.

Though men too can take on this style—a notable example being Barack Obama—women are suited to this leadership style because it greatly incorporates interpersonal skills rather than authoritarian or democratic styles that are more traditionally seen as suited to men.

Here are the five steps to take to develop a transformational approach:

1. Set and Achieve Goals

Transformational leaders are able to achieve goals by supporting the development of their team. This includes inspiring employees by being an ideal role model, using emotional intelligence when communicating, emphasizing teamwork in the workplace, and engaging with employees on a personal level. Lastly, you can achieve goals by investing a lot of your time and effort into coaching your employees. This shows them that you care about their personal development, thereby improving employee morale.

2. Avoid Transactional Leadership

As already examined in this chapter, transactional leadership can cause an atmosphere of anxiety and fear in the workplace. It sets a standard that you see your employees only as tools for the workplace's success. This is the opposite of transformational leadership, which prioritizes genuine and personal relationships with employees to inspire and motivate them to produce results in the workplace.

3. Be Fierce

Don't be afraid to be fierce. Many of us women are criticized for being opinionated and "bossy." We are termed aggressive for speaking up for what we need and want. The stereotype says that women should be demure and quiet. We are not supposed to speak up for ourselves. This stereotype limits us from our potential as bosses. Don't be afraid to take charge! You are the boss. That means that you are allowed to be bossy when needed.

Here is what Mary Barra, the CEO of General Motors, says about bossy women:

"Wherever you are in your career—your first position, or a manager, or even an executive—you have to be ready to stand up for yourself. But, it should be done in a firm but respectful way. Always remember, respect is earned. Learning to read the situation is also important. Most of all, never waver on integrity. If someone calls you bossy because you didn't let them push you around, so be it."

4. Be a Proactive Boss

An attentive leader can match employees' tasks to their strengths while allowing them to improve on their weaknesses when you feel they are ready, whether through training or added responsibility. One of the best ways to determine your employees' strengths and weaknesses is to spend personal time with them often. That way, you learn more about who they are through natural communication.

5. Communication

Communication is pivotal in every relationship. It is one of the cornerstones for building great relationships with others, even in the workplace. Women are already good at communicating because we are conditioned to over-explain our choices to others. This is a great skill to incorporate into your leadership. Good communication with your employees makes them comfortable enough to be transparent with you. They feel they can come to you to share any issues they are having in your workplace. Certainly, this will enable you to pinpoint flaws in your leadership and workplace, empowering you to implement good solutions.

Additionally, use your communication skills to praise your employees regularly. Remind them that they are essential to your workplace's success.

What Is a Situational Leader?

A situational leader is one who will adapt their leadership style depending on the situation or needs of the team. It requires the leader to adjust their skills according to their team's needs. For example, there will be times when you need to be a coach and times when you need to be transactional. There will be times when you need to be affiliative and times when you need to be bureaucratic. You will need to assess each situation to determine the appropriate style to approach it.

Situational leaders are usually successful in their workplace because they adapt to all challenges that being a leader brings. Even so, they also ensure to meet all situations with the following strengths, skills, and competencies: emotional intelligence, self-regulation, empathy, self-awareness, and motivation. Regardless of the leadership type that you may choose, you should always rely on these skills and competencies to appropriately guide you through leadership.

As a situational leader, the more leadership styles you can exhibit and integrate into your leadership, and the more flexible you are at transitioning from one to the other, the better leader you will be. Even better, the more situational your leadership becomes, the more effective your leadership will be.

Discover Your Personal Leadership Style

There is no right way to be a great leader because personality will play a part, as will your practices, actions, and values. Individual experiences matter too. For instance, if you were raised in a family where your parents/caregivers chose a coaching parenting style, you may feel more comfortable adapting a coaching style yourself. Some tips to finding your own leadership style include: being firm but flexible, doing what feels right to you and what feels suitable for the situation, spending time with your employees and learning more about them, remembering that your actions speak louder than your words, and reminding yourself that this is a process. You will not suddenly develop your personal leadership style in one go. Since we are always learning about ourselves, we are also continually learning about leadership styles.

Chapter Summary

- One of the biggest mistakes we can make is copying men's leadership styles. Instead of copying the leadership style of men, we can decide to be situational leaders.

- Situational leaders are self-aware. They know their strengths, weaknesses, and styles; they adopt these to meet different scenarios.

- As well as being a situational leader, choose to be a transformational leader. A transformational leader inspires people to work toward a common goal. They use emotional intelligence, active listening skills, supportiveness, open communication, and open-mindedness. They also engineer unity and peace.

- Don't be afraid to be bossy when you need to be. Remind yourself that women are just as qualified to take charge and to be leaders as men.

- There is no right way to be a great leader. Other factors, such as your personality, workplace practices, personal values, and individual experiences, matter too.

- Some tips for finding your personal leadership style include being firm but flexible, doing what feels right to you and suitable for the situation, and spending quality time with your employees to learn more about them.

In the next chapter, you will learn how to overcome your fear and self-doubt and believe in yourself. There are two other traits that are crucial for improving self-awareness in the area of leadership styles: being confident in yourself and improving your knowledge. The next chapter will tackle how to develop your self-confidence.

3
Overcoming Fear and Self-Doubt

"I have learned over the years that when one's mind is made up, this diminishes fear; knowing what must be done does away with fear."
Rosa Parks

There are many things to fear in a leadership role. How will people receive us? Will they accept us? How will we handle our leadership responsibilities? How do we deal with the fear of failure? If we don't overcome our fear, it will inevitably lead us to doubt our abilities.

Overcoming our fear and self-doubt is very important. It took the experience of my friend, Nadia, for me to finally understand why. After many years of hard work and training, Nadia finally reached a management position in her company. With her enthusiastic mindset and ambitious energy that could pump up even the moodiest of teams, this position was only a destiny call from how she beamed leadership potential since our active duty days. I was exceedingly proud of her for announcing when she had achieved a promotion to represent that positive prowess! It had been a long journey, and she deserved that opportunity from her hard work and dedicated growth.

Despite all this, Nadia quickly became overwhelmed by her fears. Like many, she began to battle with severe imposter syndrome. What if her company had gotten it wrong and promoted the wrong person? Did she have what it took to lead her team to success? As someone who has also dealt with fears and anxieties in leadership positions, I, amongst a group of friends, tried to encourage Nadia as much as possible. Still, it was not enough; she needed to believe in herself. Nadia felt that her self-doubt was a bad thing in and of itself. She believed that a true leader should never experience that much fear. It was a cycle, causing her to feel even more negatively about herself. She blamed herself for her feelings of fear and self-doubt, punishing herself psychologically for not being strong enough or capable enough not to have these feelings in the first place.

As women, our natural inclination is to internalize problems that come from the outside. Nadia's case was simply a normal reaction to becoming a leader. We all have these self-doubts, and while Nadia internalized her negative emotions to a worrisome degree, it was a major relief to discover that she did seek therapy to address these emotional battles. After a few months in her new position, Nadia finally began prioritizing self-care and asking for help when needed. However, many women never discover these positive pivotal realizations and simplistically healthier alternatives. Many allow this fear of failure to multiply their stress. Some refuse to take time off work for fear of appearing lazy or unproductive, creating a lack of boundaries and self-awareness. Others end up needing extensive time off because of declining mental health and increasing overwhelm, adding to the stress cycle and fear of failure. There needs to be a balance, especially during this pivotal moment in your leadership transition.

In this chapter, you will analyze how to recognize this fear, learn to believe in yourself, and understand that the problem does not lie inside you. As women, we don't have to internalize the messages that we are not good enough to be leaders. After all, it's not about fixing women; it's about fixing the biases we face that cause our deep-rooted fears. In the case of Nadia, it took a deep dive into her psyche to understand this doubtful conditioning that almost convinced her to surrender a rightfully earned achievement.

Why Female Leadership Can Bring About Fear

If you hear something over and over again, you start to believe it. This can work for good and for bad. If your parents told you repeatedly growing up that you were loved, then you would have internalized a sense of being loved and validated. If your parents criticized and questioned your ambitions, you would have internalized that a woman cannot be ambitious or be a leader. Unluckily, our brains are wired to make us more inclined to believe the negative over the positive. This is known as the negativity bias. This negativity bias only serves to strengthen our feelings of fear and self-doubt. Every day, we hear the message that we are the weaker sex and are naturally created to be quiet, timid, and shy. Women who don't follow this stereotype are not considered to be "proper ladies" and are criticized for not adhering to the stereotype of the weaker sex. Years of listening to the lie of what a proper woman is, usually beginning from childhood, leads us to doubt our own abilities. We are told that we are defined by our gender and that our gender is "the weaker sex." We are not men, who are told that they are natural leaders, fighters, warriors, and kings. Consequently, when women achieve leadership, we don't have that voice inside us telling us that we deserve the position. Instead, our inner voice tells us that we are undeserving and will make bad leaders.

To an extent, much of our fear comes from listening to the bias surrounding women in power. Some of these we have already covered. It's very much a double bind. We can't be bossy or outspoken as a leader, but at the same time, we can't be seen as weak. Essentially, we are going to be criticized no matter what we decide to do. So, women may struggle with discovering the right balance. Fear also comes from the bias surrounding women and families. Even today, the primary expectation for women is to raise the family. There is the assumption that careers come second, or as something to indulge in casually, before returning to their "natural" job as caretakers.

Women may also be highly encouraged and expected to pursue nurturing career options, such as nurses and teachers but discouraged and criticized more from lead roles such as doctors or principals. Therefore, we fear stepping out of our comfort zones. Finally, depending on the industry, there is the question of physical strength and stamina. One woman may have a passion for construction but fear going for her goals in an industry that is dominated by presumingly strong men. We know that, logically, this shouldn't be the case as not all men are stronger than all women, but it's still a societal bias that we all unconsciously buy into, regardless of our gender.

Here is what Environment and Health consultant at Ramboll, Christine B. Ng, says about this (Ramboll, 2022):

> *"Speaking from my own childhood and young adult experience, I was often discouraged by my family and other trusted people from taking risks, which I've found to be a common thread for other girls and women. I accepted and excelled at tasks asked of me, but these tended to be within my comfort zone. That meant waiting to respond to a teacher's questions until I was 100% certain of the answer, hesitating to be critical of someone in charge,*

or taking on an assignment or role only if I was confident of success.

This also led others to think I would excel in 'safe' opportunities but would not be eager to pursue 'high risk, high reward' pursuits. Over the years, first as an engineering student decades ago and now as a Principal at Ramboll, I've tried to push past my inherent risk aversion while taking on new challenges, which has been stressful but rewarding. We can support the girls and women in our lives by encouraging them to take risks that could advance their education, career, and personal growth, and appreciate that we can learn as much from failure as success."

As much as we fear failure, we can also fear success. Reaching success (as in becoming a leader) isn't the end goal. You then have to maintain this success. Women achieving positions of power is still seen as an oddity in every society in the world today. You can see this by the fact that we're still establishing "The First Woman" title today. The first woman to take a certain role, and the first woman of color, is seen as "historic." As a result, when women make it into leadership positions, the spotlight is on them. People want to know how we will deal with this responsibility. Since women are stereotyped as not being suited for positions of leadership, people watch every move women leaders make.

Women in leadership positions are conscious of the fact that people are preoccupied with whether they succeed or fail. Naturally, this adds to the pressure that women in these positions feel. Rather than enjoy our success, we actually feel as though we are only actors on a stage, with people waiting intently for our failure. This fear of failure and success can hold women back.

How to Overcome Anxiety and Fear of Leadership

Here are some wonderful steps for overcoming anxiety and fear of leadership:

Acknowledge Your Feelings

It is absolutely okay to feel anxious, fearful, and overwhelmed at times. These are feelings that are as natural as any other human emotions. One of the ways in which leadership has traditionally worked is that emotions have been suppressed in favor of stoicism. It's a wonderful thing that, as women enter into more leadership positions, we can change this idea that emotions are inherently "wrong." Emotions are natural. They are there to guide us on what is good for us and what isn't. When you're angry, it is your psyche's way of telling you that something is amiss.

Listen to your emotions. Just because leaders are often portrayed as calm, collected Mad Men-type figures who never let their emotions get to them does not mean that this is necessarily true. We are all human, and workplace-related stress will always eventually take a toll on your mental health. This is why many people in leadership positions often eventually succumb to unhealthy coping mechanisms, such as addiction. These coping mechanisms also negatively affect their lives at home. Before it gets to this stage, acknowledge your emotions. Say to yourself, "I feel anxious, but this is okay. How can I healthily cope with this anxiety?" Coping strategies, such as yoga, pilates, baking, cooking, meditation, knitting, running, spending time with family and friends, volunteer work, gaming, dancing, and so on, are great ways to relieve stress and keep your mental health in tip-top condition.

Understand Your Triggers

Before your anxiety gets the best of you, you can take control of the process by understanding what triggers you. Different situations trigger our anxiety because we all have different personalities and past experiences. For example, you may get triggered when things are not well-planned. Other people get triggered when things are *too* planned because they have a more laissez-faire attitude toward life. Take the time to examine your reactions to different environments and situations. By becoming self-aware, you learn what triggers you, giving you the upper hand in preventing anxiety before it has a chance to overwhelm you. Once you spot that a situation or an environment triggers you, take the time to reassure yourself that you can do this. Tell yourself that this is only a challenge to help you grow so you can face your triggers without them overwhelming you.

Change Your Mental Attitude

I must admit, it can be daunting to think about how achieving your goals only puts you in the spotlight. It seems all our flaws are even more greatly emphasized when people are paying attention to us. I want to challenge you to change your mental attitude. As women, if we want to make the idea of women leaders become an accepted norm, we must be prepared to face the challenges that spring forth. This includes the challenge of being in the spotlight.

It is never easy, but Sandra Day O'Connor, former US Supreme Court Justice, gives us a great way to handle the pressure of being in the spotlight. She explains:

> "For both men and women, the first step in getting power is to become visible to others—and then to put on an impressive show. The acquisition of power requires that one aspire to power, that one believe power is possible. As women then achieve power and exercise it well, the barriers fall. That's why I'm optimistic. As society sees what women can do, as women see what women can do, there will be even more women out there doing things—and we'll all be better off for it. Certainly today women should be optimistically encouraged to exercise their power and their leadership skills wherever it might take them."

Think of the spotlight not as a reason to shrink from responsibility and the public eye. Rather, think of it as O'Connor prefers to: the spotlight is a chance for you to show other women and girls who aspire to be leaders that they can do it. I guarantee you that men who achieve leadership status also face fears and self-doubt. I believe that removing the pressure of thinking you must succeed because you are one of the first women to enter leadership will help you to simply enjoy the process. I would go as far as to say that you are also allowed to fail. Millions of men who have gone before you have failed, so why must you be chastised when something as human as failure happens to you? Remind yourself that you got this position because you are worthy; if you fail, it is because you are only human. Failure is your opportunity to improve. Learn from your mistakes, and come back stronger.

Know That You Can Rewire Your Brain's Negativity

One of the most amazing things about the human brain is that we can rewire it to work as we want it to. Although our brain may be wired toward negativity, we can rewire it toward positivity if we want to. We can make our brain more adept at carrying out challenging tasks. The ability to change how our brain works is called neuroplasticity. Neuroplasticity is a field in science that studies how the brain changes based on everyday stimuli. That means that you can rewire your brain to be less anxious and to be able to thrive in a leadership role. Since anxiety and fear are emotions we have spent years building through repeated thought patterns and behavior, we can rewire our brain toward positivity using the same repeated thought patterns and behavior. While you might have repeatedly told yourself that you couldn't do something, prompting fear and anxiety to take over your life, you can repeatedly tell yourself that you are indeed capable of achieving success. You can rewire your brain into the brain of a leader.

Michele Buck, CEO of Hershey's, said:

> *"Make an impact in every single assignment that you are given. Look at it as how can I take this to the next level. And be confident in yourself. I think women just don't have as much inherent confidence in themselves. They tend to be harsher critics of themselves than they need to be. So go for it."*

If You Doubt Your Skills, So Will Your Team

Imposter syndrome is a psychological occurrence when someone doubts their abilities to the extent that they feel like a fraud. For example, you have earned your promotion, but now that you are there, you don't feel like you deserve it. Gender bias and "boy's club" exclusion only make self-doubt in female leaders worse. And just because a male co-worker is more confident than you doesn't mean they are more competent.

Self-doubt has a habit of sabotaging leadership. No matter how much you try to hide it, employees will notice if you don't believe in yourself as a leader. This will undermine your authority. Any honest leader, male or female, will tell you that they have had moments when they doubted their abilities. This is completely normal. What is important is how you handle your self-doubt. As well as neuroplasticity, another useful strategy for dealing with self-doubt is to break the cycle so it doesn't spiral out of control. To do this, you can:

Give Yourself Twenty-Four Hours, Then Get Over It

It's healthy to give yourself time to feel bad for yourself. Sometimes we get things wrong, and sometimes we encounter situations that only serve to drive our self-doubt. Give yourself twenty-four hours to feel bad. I like to think of these twenty-four hours as a mini grieving period. The next day, you can start over again, ready to take on the leadership challenge once more.

Remember, People Don't Care as Much as You Think

A lot of our self-doubt comes from those little mistakes that we pay more attention to than others. You may have messed up a slide in your presentation—but nobody remembers that because the rest of your presentation was awesome. Even if they did notice, people generally don't care because they're also deep in their own lives, just as you are.

Role-Play Your Insecurities

Role-playing your insecurities is a great way to remove the power your insecurities have over you. You can role-play by pretending that you are a friend listening to you vocalize your insecurities. Do so by recording yourself speaking to your friend, then play it back and listen intently as a caring friend would. You'll soon hear that many of your insecurities are overreactions created out of self-doubt. Doing this gives you the ability to perceive your negative thoughts from a more compassionate perspective. It helps you to understand that your insecurities do not define you, and you don't have to let them overpower you.

Vent in a Healthy Way

Venting to friends and family is a great way to work through your self-doubt. Talk to people you trust about your insecurities so they can remind you of all the ways in which you are awesome and deserve to be a leader. The only caveat is to make sure you choose friends and families who have been supportive, compassionate, and encouraging in the past.

Find a Distraction

Negative thoughts can keep us in a spiral of despair. Don't give into despair. Seek distractions that are pleasurable, and focus your attention away from your negative spiral. Watch a comedy, go for a run, read a book, spend quality time with your family and friends, or participate in any other form of distraction. Distractions, when used in moderation, help break the cycle of despair, giving you time to recharge and move back into leadership from a place of strength and positivity.

Chapter Summary

- Overcoming our fear and self-doubt is important if we want to be successful leaders.

- Negativity bias strengthens our feelings of fear and self-doubt as women. A lot of our fear comes from listening to this bias.

- As much as we fear failure, we also fear success because

of the responsibilities that it brings.

- You can rewire your brain's negativity, moving your brain from anxiety and self-doubt into confidence and happiness.

In the next chapter, you will learn the seven hard skills and how you can improve these skills in your new leadership role. You will also learn the importance of having the right knowledge to be a leader and, ultimately, feeling confident in your role.

4
Why Hard Skills Are Essential for Leaders

"The most difficult thing is the decision to act, the rest is merely tenacity."
Amelia Earhart

When looking at hard skills and soft skills, I am always reminded of Mrs. Doubtfire. She (pretending to be a nanny) had all the necessary soft skills to excel in the job, but when it came to the hard skills required to run the home, she was pretty lost. You can develop hard skills through education and practice, often with a kind of qualification or certificate that can be listed on a resume. They require time and dedication to master, and what's more, they require continuous training to retain the knowledge gained, as well as the level of skills gained. Mrs. Doubtfire failed because she could not pick up those hard skills on the job.

Hard skills are the technical skills we have that are quantifiable. Basically, they are skills that you acquired through training, education, experience at work, reading, and so on. They are skills that you can easily be tested on. Soft skills are the opposite. They are much more difficult to quantify because they are qualitative interpersonal skills that you use to communicate and develop a relationship with others. Examples of soft skills include communication, work ethic, and stress management skills.

Another significant difference between hard and soft skills is that soft skills are generally valued across all roles and all industries. As you can imagine, hard skills can be industry-specific. A woman wanting to run her own car mechanic business will need a different set of hard skills (mechanical skills) compared with a woman who wants to start a software company (technological skills). Nonetheless, they will also need roughly the same soft skills if they want to thrive in business. Both women will need to be able to communicate with respect and compassion if they want to keep employee retention high. They will also need to be able to communicate well with customers if they want their business to run smoothly.

As women, we're often expected to excel in soft skills. We've all heard the stereotypes that women are naturally good at relationships, caring for others, and keeping families and friendships together. On the flip side, we also have to battle the myth that women cannot possibly possess hard skills. Industries that require hard skills have traditionally been dominated by men because women were often not allowed to pursue education in many of these fields, such as technology, medicine, finance, politics, and so on. One obvious example is Marie Curie, who only won the Nobel Peace Prize after her husband insisted that he would not accept his prize unless her scientific efforts were recognized too.

We've all had experiences where we were shunned, ostracized, humiliated, or punished for not displaying soft skills or for displaying hard skills. We are told repeatedly that our worth is in our interpersonal skills, while any hard skills we acquire make us less worthy of love and respect from others. Yet, as you've learned in previous chapters, we're all individuals. The sexist stereotype that all women are the same is a major stumbling block in most women's lives because people make untrue assumptions about our personalities, characteristics, and skills. Don't allow people to force you into a box of their own limitations. Your unique combination of hard and soft skills are what makes you, well you. They empower you to thrive in your own personal leadership style, turning you into an efficient and successful leader! Likewise, acquiring hard skills does not make you any less worthy or loveable as a woman.

Seven Transferable Hard Skills

In many cases, to be taken seriously as a leader, you have to be able to prove your hard skills. So, what are the seven main types of hard skills and how can we improve them?

1. Management Skills

Managerial skills are essential for all industries and companies. Companies with strong managers earn higher profits and see greater productivity and higher employee engagement. When you show great managerial skills, you directly, but non-verbally, communicate to your employees and your employers that you know what you are doing. People are more prone to trusting and following leaders who have great management skills, so let's go through the six methods you can use to improve your management skills.

Be Self-Aware and Self-Reflective

Managers who are self-aware are managers who are emotionally intelligent. Emotional intelligence can only be developed through regular introspection and honest evaluation of your strengths, your weaknesses, and your failures. For example, spending each day reflecting on what you did right and what you did wrong enables you to develop better skills and managerial responses. This, in turn, promotes a well-run workplace where your employees feel cared for, respected, and safe. According to Harvard Business School (Gavin, 2020):

> "In one study by Harvard Business School professors Francesca Gino and Gary Pisano, it was found that call center employees who spent 15 minutes reflecting at the end of the workday performed 23 percent better after 10 days than those who did not."

In the same article, HBS Professor Amy Edmondson says:

> "If we don't have the time and space to reflect on what we're doing and how we're doing it, we can't learn. In so many organizations today, people just feel overly busy. They're going 24/7 and think, 'I don't have time to reflect.' That's a huge mistake, because if you don't have time to reflect, you don't have time to learn. You're going to quickly be obsolete. People need the self-discipline and the collective discipline to make time to reflect."

Self-reflection brings greater self-awareness. We've already discussed how knowing yourself enables you to understand your triggers, giving you the skills to be better able to emotionally regulate in the workplace. No employee wants to work for a manager who cannot control their emotions and cannot make decisions because they feel too anxious or fearful at the moment.

Provide Trust

People work best for managers who they trust. Your employees will be better engaged at work when they feel they can trust you to make the right decisions and support them when they need it. When you build trust, you can forge deeper connections with your employees. Humans love to feel connected. It gives your employees renewed energy for work and reduces stress. You can build trust by engaging with your employees on a personal level, for example, by asking them about their lives outside of work. Another way to build trust is to be open-minded, creating a happy environment where employees feel that they can talk to you about anything without judgment or blowback.

Employ Good Decision-Making

An effective manager knows how to make effective decisions. This is not to say that every decision you make will be the exact right one; however, your employees need to know that you can examine complex workplace problems and implement a plan for solving these problems and moving forward. Decision-making skills need years of experience to hone. Another way to sharpen your decision-making skills is to take online courses for leaders.

Communicate

Communication is the central building block of any relationship, including that of a leader and their team members. You need to be able to communicate with your employees to give them the right tools and information to succeed. Bad communication will easily destroy a team. In the next chapter, you will learn how to improve your communication skills.

Utilize Feedback and Regular Check-Ins

Regular check-ins and feedback are a great way to build interpersonal relationships with your team members. It is a common strategy used in all forms of relationships because it allows you to discuss the areas in your relationship/team that is doing well and address areas that could use improvements. As a leader, regular check-ins, incorporated with the emotional intelligence to deliver negative feedback in a way that is palatable to your employees, will affirm your role as a trustworthy leader.

Implement Regular Training

A progressive leader needs continuous training, not just in decision-making skills, but in every area of leadership. Regular training allows you to learn new techniques, tools, and skills that will improve your leadership processes to the advantage of you, your team, and your organization. Regular training is also a great way to network with your peers and gain insight into different perspectives and backgrounds that you may not personally have around you. This will then inform your managerial approach, helping you to be better suited to lead people from various backgrounds. It is an invaluable tool for professional growth.

2. Computer Skills

In today's world, you aren't going to get far without computer skills. Some skills will be specific to a company, depending on the software used. In general, leaders should have a solid grasp of spreadsheets, social media, email, graphic design, word processing, and those areas that come up under troubleshooting.

You also need regular training to enhance and improve your computer skills since the technological world is constantly advancing. The best way to determine which skills you need to master is to research your industry, taking detailed notes of what software and computer skills are in demand.

3. Project Management Skills

Project management requires a set of skills for planning, initiating, and completing tasks to reach a goal. The ability to prioritize, use project management software, and be proactive are some of the skills you need for project management. These skills depend greatly on three major skills: organizational, time management, and communication. Organizational skills allow you to prioritize the most important skills first, giving the least important tasks the least prioritization. This works best with time management skills to ensure you dedicate time to each task efficiently. Lastly, you need communication to be able to facilitate the smooth running of any project with more than one person on the team.

4. Human Resources Skills

Because of the fast-changing pace in HR, this is one area where it's important to keep up with regular training to stay updated. HR skills that you will rely on as a leader include strategic thinking, people management, and delegation. HR skills are also essential for learning how to run an effective organization that enables people from all walks of life, regardless of gender, religion, culture, ethnicity, race, sexuality, and so on, to feel welcome under your leadership. Never forget that the more diverse your team is, the wider pool of talent you can accumulate. You are a personal example of this phenomenon because you are able to bring a distinct form of leadership as a woman that a man may not be able to bring.

5. Strategic Planning Skills

Strategic planning is the practice of defining future strategies. Strategic planning skills allow you to develop other business designs, create templates, negotiate and sell, present ideas, and create bridges among departments.

6. Marketing Skills

Marketing in a data-driven world requires a knowledge of statistics, budgets, and return-on-investment along with building strong relationships through various forms of digital connectivity. It helps to know enough about effective marketing strategies to influence your ideas and solutions for presentation to your team and managers.

7. Analytical Skills

You must develop intuitive decision-making and reasoning skills (based on logic). Analytical skills are a great tool for any leader because they allow you to take in as much information as possible to make informed, data-backed decisions. This helps you make effective decisions. You're also more likely to learn from your mistakes and the mistakes of others and apply that knowledge to new situations.

You also need to be knowledgeable in tools like Google Analytics, which analyzes internet data to enable you to choose how to promote your online workspace or business better.

The great news about technology today is that we have access to an arsenal of free courses online that can improve our skills and, even better, that cost little compared to traditional learning methods. Flexibility with online learning means we can fit them in with our current responsibilities; it is a great place to start.

Admittedly, continuously learning is a challenge. If it was easy, most people would do it. On those days when I know that I must work on improving my skills, but I don't want to because it's difficult, I remember the wise words of Indra Nooyi, former CEO of PepsiCo:

> *"Just because you are CEO, don't think you have landed. You must continually increase your learning, the way you think, and the way you approach the organization. I've never forgotten that."*

There is always room for growth. If you're not growing, you're stagnating; if you are stagnating, you are regressing. You see this phenomenon in many CEOs today who stop putting any effort into their growth once they reach the position they've worked decades to achieve. This affects their company negatively because their lack of personal and skill growth is reflected in their organizational practices.

Industries are constantly changing and growing. In fact, the concept of growth applies to most things in life. As a result, you can never afford to stay stagnant—your industry, your community, your family, your friends, and even the world will leave you behind in your state of regression.

Chapter Summary

- You can develop hard skills through education and practice, often with a certificate that can be listed on a resume. They require time and dedication to master and continuous training to retain the knowledge gained.

- Soft skills are qualitative interpersonal skills that you use to communicate and develop relationships with others.

- Soft skills are generally valued across all roles and all industries, while hard skills can be industry-specific.

- As women, we have to battle with the myth that we cannot possibly possess hard skills. We are told that hard skills we acquire make us less worthy of love and respect from others.

- Do not allow people to force you into a box of their own

limitations. To be taken seriously as a leader, you have to be able to prove your hard skills.

- Hard skills are such that you can continue developing them no matter what stage of your leadership career.

In the next chapter, you will learn how to find your voice and use practical communication skills to empower the leader you are.

5
Finding Your Voice and Making It Heard

"A woman with a voice is by definition a strong woman. But the search to find that voice can be remarkably difficult."
Melinda Gates

Now that you understand the hard skills that you need to be an effective leader, you can now focus on the most important soft skill you need to be an effective leader: communication. This chapter will also touch upon related soft skills like teamwork, solving problems as a group, delegation, and creating expectations and professional boundaries.

One thing I've noticed that cuts across many cultures, genders, and societies is that most of us are not taught how to appropriately, actively, and effectively communicate. Communication is a field in itself, and millions of books have been written on how to communicate. This is because communication is multifaceted and an exceedingly useful skill to have regardless of who you are or what you do. Jim Rohn put it aptly when he said:

> *"Take advantage of every opportunity to practice your communication skills so that when im-*

portant occasions arise, you will have the gift, the sharpness, the clarity, and the emotions to affect other people."

You can get out of sticky situations through communication. Communication is what will win you that life-changing contract. Your communication skills are what will convince a college to admit you into that prestigious program. In so many ways, the way we communicate determines the course of our lives and whether the life path that we take will lead to greater success or not. So, how can women leaders use communication as a tool toward success?

The Gender Bias Lives On

Contrary to popular belief, in the workplace, men tend to talk more while women are regularly interrupted. Even worse, because men are more likely to speak up in meetings and suggest ideas, they automatically become more visible in the workplace, giving them a greater chance of being promoted into leadership positions. Studies show that men who talk more are seen as 10% more competent, while women who do the same are viewed as 14% less competent (Bay Area Council, 2017). Women are also more likely to not only be interrupted but also to be given less credit for their ideas. Of this, Madeleine Albright, the former US Secretary of State, said:

"I have often been the only woman in the room and I thought to myself, 'Well, I don't think I'll say anything today because it'll sound stupid,'

> and then some man says it and everyone thinks it's brilliant and you think, 'Why didn't I talk?' If we are in a meeting, we're there for a reason. ==The bottom line is if you're only there, not speaking you kind of create the impression that you're not prepared to be there.=="

As with most things, women are damned if we do and damned if we don't. This is exactly why Madeleine Albright is adamant that we might as well do. You might as well take the chance so you can reap the benefit of your risk paying off. A motivational leader is one who is not afraid of taking risks. Rather than staying quiet, a better strategy is to speak out, while understanding the blowback you might receive because you are breaking out of the stereotype of how a "good woman" should behave. Indeed, educating yourself on how you might be perceived when you speak out gives you a better understanding of dealing with the negative consequences of finding your voice.

You must also take into account that men and women have different communication styles and judge others from their preferred method of communication. Understanding gendered styles of communication enable you to meet people on their own turf, reducing your chances of tension between team members. In general, one major difference between men and women is relationship orientation. In quick summary, relationship orientation breaks down that women are focused on relationships and men are focused on tasks. Generally, women prefer to first develop a relationship and then to use that relationship to work collaboratively, but men experience frustration with this method. Generally, men use tasks as a means to connect with others.

This doesn't mean that all men and all women work exactly alike. If you lean on the side of relationship-oriented communication, you can switch your style to become more task-oriented when you meet people who prefer task-oriented communication, and vice versa. This presents you as a situational leader, earning you the respect of those around you.

When it comes to making decisions, men also generally tend to process their thoughts internally before making a decision, while women tend to ask others for advice before making a decision. This can cause conflict because women may interpret a man's silence while he is processing an issue as disinterest. Since men are typically socialized to believe that asking for help is the sign of weakness, it's most likely that the man around you will not want to ask for help when making a decision.

Another difference is in non-verbal communication. Women tend to use non-verbal communication to show that they are listening to the other party—things like nodding, eye contact, and smiling. Men, on the other hand, tend to stand still when listening. This can be misinterpreted as a lack of interest in the conversation. Women in this position tend to want to engage the man by repeating themselves or trying to entice the man back into the conversation. This only serves to make the man feel frustrated.

There is also unequal engagement. Men tend to provide information without really seeking information. They generally believe it is their duty to dominate conversations, resulting in talking over or interrupting the women. They are more focused on demonstrating primary verbal dominion in groups, while women are more focused on giving everyone an opportunity to speak. It is quite common for women to opt out of a conversation or simply stop speaking when they feel a man is dominating the conversation and interrupting them.

Understanding Effective Communication

Effective communication isn't just about how you speak. It's how you deliver and receive information, be it written, verbal, in listening, or through body language. If you deliver criticism to one of your employees while standing with your arms crossed, they likely will take this criticism hard. What should've been constructive feedback to enable them to improve on the work only serves to cripple them mentally, so they begin to produce shoddy work. Comparatively, if you give constructive criticism while sitting next to them and after inquiring about the well-being of their family, your employer is likely to reflect on the criticism you've given them and put effort into improving. As people often say, it is not what you say but how you say it.

Here are ten ways to improve communication skills:

1. Actively Listen

Most people don't carefully listen when others are speaking to them. Most of the time, people are simply waiting for a turn to speak. Often, people don't even wait and interrupt. Active listening involves carving out space mentally, emotionally, and physically to take in everything that the other person is communicating to you, both verbally and non-verbally. Do they sound sad when they tell you about their pet, even though they are trying to seem upbeat? Do you notice a nervous tone when they tell you about a particular event they swore was resolved? What are they inferring when they say certain things? That is, what are they leaving out and why are they leaving out that message? There is so much information to glean when you actively listen.

2. Understand Your Non-Verbal Communication

Non-verbal communication is a language of its own. Entire books have been written on this topic because society has developed a complex language using only non-verbal signals. To make things even more complicated, different cultures sometimes use different meanings when portraying the same non-verbal cues. Unfortunately, we won't be able to cover every way you can interpret or misinterpret non-verbal cues in this book. Think of non-verbal communication as training to take on your own time to improve your leadership skills. Don't be daunted by the idea of non-verbal communication being a language on its own; we generally understand the basics inherently. We can tell when someone is angry and when someone is a threat to us without the person speaking a word. We unconsciously learn non-verbal communication in childhood. It does, nevertheless, help to turn what is an unconscious process into a conscious understanding by studying non-verbal communication and learning how to decipher it.

One other trick that works for me is being aware of my entrance. Have you ever stopped to watch an important man in business attire make an entrance? He is self-assured, with his shoulders back and confidently making eye contact with everyone in the room. He doesn't try to make himself look small or to take up as little space as possible. You need to have a presence when you enter a space. You want people to read your body language as confident and ready to lead. You want people to have faith that they can come to you with any problem and you will provide guidance.

3. Provide Clear Instructions in Your Communication

Say what you mean and mean what you say. Be clear and direct in your communication so that others don't have the opportunity to misunderstand you. Verify that the instructions are simplified and comprehensible. If they are not, be empathetic and explain it differently to help your team understand it better. Misunderstandings can be costly and damaging to your relationships, so you want to avoid this whenever possible.

4. Master Your Stress and Anxiety

A well-grounded leader needs to understand how to keep stress and anxiety from affecting their work and leadership. Your communication skills suffer when stress and anxiety get the best of you. We also often lose patience when we are stressed. Your anxiety may cause you to write an unclear email with ambiguous directions rather than clear and concise instructions. To avoid unintended reactions, it's best to learn how to master your stress and anxiety in ways that work for you as an individual.

5. Show Empathy

Empathy goes a long way. Maya Angelou said,

> *"I've learned that people will forget what you said, people will forget what you did, but people will never forget how you made them feel."*

You can either become a person who leaves behind positive memorable information and associations with others, or you can leave your team feeling negative about themselves. You must learn how to communicate with empathy and compassion. As we've seen in the sample of both methods of giving criticism to employees, a leader who does not exercise empathy is bound to fail.

6. Inform the Team

Informative communication does not mean bombarding your team with a pile of random updates from every department; rather, it means understanding what information your team needs to thrive and presenting that in a timely, straightforward manner. Providing too much irrelevant information will eventually cause your team to ignore your updates. Connect with your team's needs and provide the resolution.

7. Complete Your Instructions

It is unprofessional if you do not provide complete instructions to your team. Assuming that they'll "figure it out" can invoke unnecessary stress and decreased trust in your capabilities to lead the project. This lack of completion can also cause misinformation among your team, ultimately leading to chaos and failure. Understand that what might be obvious to you might not be obvious to the rest of your team.

8. Give and Receive Feedback
A diligent leader uses feedback as a tool for improvement. This includes giving and receiving constructive criticism and empowering your employees to make changes by providing them with the resources and agency to do so. Don't be afraid to receive feedback from your team. They work closest to you and know you better than most people. That means they have invaluable information on how you can improve your work.

9. Use Your Time Wisely
A leader who values their time will use their time wisely. One good strategy I have learned is to occasionally join community activities like mini game sessions with some of my employees on Zoom. That way, I can enjoy a fun break while learning more about my team and building stronger connectivity with them.

10. Provide Visuals
Humans collect information through the five senses, of which vision and hearing collect the most. You can convey a lot of information through vision, so do not be afraid to use it when communicating with others. You may be surprised to that 90% of human communication is non-verbal (The University of Texas, 2022). That means that most of the information we get from others are hand gestures, body movements, colors and patterns, and read-between-the-lines information that is left unsaid. Think about the first thing you do when you meet a new person. You take them in and make a first impression of them based entirely on what you see. Vision is an important sense for how we navigate the world, so don't be afraid to use visual aids,

such as charts, graphs, and pictures, when communicating with others.

Getting Your Words Right

There is no need for blanket or "fluff" words in leadership roles. Filler words such as "like," "basically," "um," and "hmm" delete meaning and distract from the power of your words. We often add fillers to the beginning or end of a sentence or between the pauses without noticing it. We either lose track of our words or lose confidence in what we are saying.

We women give away our power through the way we speak without even realizing it. From childhood, we are told off or punished when we are more direct with our speech. We're called "sassy," "rude," or "disrespectful." We get in trouble at school and at home for being confidently direct in our speech and not showing enough deference. This ties back to the idea of women being seen as aggressive instead of assertive. To combat this, we learn early on in childhood to use the way we speak to imply deference to others. We try to show that we are "good" girls by being excessively collaborative at the expense of our boundaries.

Another common way in which women give our power away is by apologizing. We often apologize for things beyond our control or things that we are not responsible for. Let me give you an example. Your coworker joins a virtual meeting with you on time to discuss the progress of a project, and the first thing she says upon joining is, "Sorry if I sound tired." This immediately demonstrates a submissive state and a lack of confidence that you value yourself.

Another way we show deference is by hedging. In linguistics, hedging is when you use a word or phrase that shows ambiguity or uncertainty. You may say "I feel as if I would be a good fit for this role." This differs from saying, "I would make a great fit for this role." Immediately, you can see the difference in how you may be perceived when you use a hedge in a sentence. You are seen as less confident in your abilities and in yourself. You give off the message that you have no self-assurance. In a cutthroat world where leaders are expected to be decisive, hedging removes that power.

As with everything else, it all boils down to your neuroplasticity. If you have taught your brain to speak in a manner that shows subservience, it will take time and conscious practice to transition into more power-oriented speech. This is still achievable. You can do it. Start small. You may be at the coffee shop and find yourself asking, "Sorry, but can I have a cupcake?" Once you notice this, you can reiterate your question by stating: "I would like a cupcake, please." Small changes in your language, made incrementally over time, will eventually have you tapping into your linguistic power.

Lastly, always take the information you know and process it to provide what needs to be heard, not what people want or pressure you to say. Before long, you will find the power in your voice.

As women, we tend to focus on how to change our voice, quieting it as a way to deliver bad news or to soften a blow, but there is more to the power of our voice than this. The power of your voice has multiple uses. If you watch videos of some of history's greatest orators, you will see that they use their voice, volume, cadence, and confidence to incite their followers: some for good and some for bad. They speak from their gut (not their upper chest), finding the power from within without coming across as aggressive.

Completing the Communication Package

I recommend the PREP method to help women be heard in a male-dominated environment. The PREP framework is an effective tool to use when you need to communicate with conviction and confidence. It stands for Point, Reason, Example, Point:

Point

Start your communication with your point. This enables you to establish your topic. It is better to stick to one point or as few as possible to keep your audience's attention. If you have many points, use the PREP framework in a series to establish different topics. An example of a point is to say: "We can beat last week's target of feeding 100 children."

Reason

What is your reason for making your point? A reason displays that you have given your point adequate thought, validating your claim(s). An example for the point above is to say: "If we stay open an hour later, we give children coming from schools far away more time to get here."

Example

Give some examples that justify the truth of your point. Facts, statistics, and personal experience can all illustrate your point. An example is to explain: "Last Friday, we spoke with parents whose children attend schools outside of this district, and they informed us that it takes them a while to get here because of traffic at that time. We also spoke to some of the older students from the nearby schools who told us they like hanging out here after school; they don't mind waiting about thirty minutes to an hour to help out—especially if we provide a few extra snacks for them to take home."

Point

Reiterate your point so it sticks in your audience's mind. If you have any other arguments that prove your point, you can add them here. An example is to state: "Let's not forget that the meal many of these children receive is the only nutritious and healthy meal they will receive all day. If we can feed more children, we will do something great for them and the community."

Networking

The importance of networking should never go unnoticed. Traditionally, networking is about creating contacts in your field. For women, this can also be an opportunity to connect with other strong leaders like yourself to build a better support system and share ideas. Here are some popular female leadership networks to guide you in your journey to becoming your best you:

21Ninety
Allbright
Asian Indigenous Women's Network
Black Career Women's Network
Black Women Networking
Bloomsbury Beginnings
Boss Babe Academy
ColorComm
DrivenWoman

<u>Entrepreneurship Latina Leaders of America</u>
<u>Everywoman</u>
<u>Forward Ladies</u>
<u>HeyMama</u>
<u>Hispanic Alliance for Career Advancement</u>
<u>Hub Dot</u>
<u>Lean in Circles</u>
<u>Mothers Meeting</u>
<u>National Black Women's Network</u>
<u>Native Action Network</u>
<u>Native Women Lead</u>
<u>Northern Power Women</u>
<u>Peanut</u>
<u>PowHERful Foundation</u>
<u>ProjectWE</u>
<u>PurposeGirls: The Women's Happiness Network</u>
<u>The Entreprenista League</u>
<u>The Wing</u>
<u>We Are the City</u>
<u>Women in Business Network</u>
<u>Women Who Startup</u>

In this chapter, you have learned the importance of finding your voice. One important thing to take away from this chapter is that your voice is one of your most essential tools for achieving and retaining power. Never stifle it. You will often feel pressured to give in and give up by swallowing your words down, but you must never do that. Instead, when that pressure gets to you, remember these wise words by the philanthropist, Melinda Gates:

> "To me, empowerment means if a woman has her voice and her agency. Can she say what she thinks needs to be said in any setting? Does she have the agency to make decisions on behalf of herself and her family? If you sit on a corporate board and you don't think you can

voice what you're seeing on that board or in that corporation that is wrong, then you don't have your voice ... When a woman in the US gets on a corporate board, when there's one of her, she's not going to make a change. When there are two or three, then she has agency and she has her voice because there's a power in the collective. Then they get the other men on the board with her who are also saying, 'Hey, we're seeing the same things,' and they come forward as a group. There's a power in the collective of the group. Men have had these natural networks for a long time. Women have tons of social networks, but it's not until you get them together, and get them together in the right way, that they give women their voice and their agency."

Chapter Summary

- Most women are not taught how to appropriately, actively, and effectively communicate.

- When you're able to understand gendered styles of communication, it enables you to meet people on their own turf.

- Men and women tend to have different communication styles. This can lead to miscommunication between genders.

- You use effective communication as a tool for successful leadership.

- You can take back your power as a woman through

verbal and non-verbal communication.

- Use the PREP method to help you be heard in a male-dominated environment.

- Don't underestimate the importance of networking for creating contacts in your field and for creating contacts within female leadership.

- By building your network, you build a better support system around you with which you can share ideas.

In the next chapter, you will learn why emotional intelligence is crucial for leadership roles and why it is one of the greatest reasons women make such excellent leaders.

Emotional Intelligence and Its Role in Leadership

> *"Don't be intimidated by what you don't know. That can be your greatest strength and ensure that you do things differently from everyone else."*
> Sara Blakely

Emotional intelligence seems to be one of those phrases thrown around these days, but what does it mean exactly? As the name suggests, it is just simply being intelligent emotionally. In a previous chapter, you learned how emotions are a big part of human life. It is crucial to understand how to navigate not just your own emotions but also the emotions of others. I like this concise definition of emotional intelligence (Mayer and Salovey, 1997) that states that it is:

> *"the ability to perceive accurately, appraise, and express emotion; the ability to access and/or generate feelings when they facilitate thought; the ability to understand emotion and emotional knowledge; and the ability to regulate emotions to promote emotional and intellectual growth."*

Emotional intelligence gives us the understanding and ability to monitor our and others' feelings, evaluate where these emotions come from, and decipher what events caused these emotions to arise in the first place. We can also use this information to guide our next moves and thoughts. Likewise, emotional intelligence is the tool that we use to regulate our emotions and allow people to help others to regulate their own emotions too.

Also known as EQ, emotional intelligence gives you the ability to recognize, understand and manage your own emotions and recognize, understand, and influence the emotions of others. It is a necessary part of leadership because it helps give and receive feedback, meet deadlines, deal with challenging people, cope with change, and overcome setbacks. EQ allows for better conflict resolution, training, motivation, and collaboration. Studies from Harvard Business School show that EQ could be twice as important as IQ (IHHP, 2022). Women tend to make excellent leaders because of how they engage with emotional intelligence. According to Meshkat and Nejati (2017), there is:

> "no significant difference between the genders on their total score measuring emotional intelligence, but the genders did tend to differ in emotional self-awareness, interpersonal relationship, self-regard, and empathy, with females scoring higher than males."

These skills—self-awareness, interpersonal relationships, self-regard, and empathy—are soft skills that, as you have seen in this book, improve leadership significantly. As transformational leadership (a popular style among female leaders) is highly linked to emotional intelligence, we can see why women make such excellent leaders. So, why is emotional intelligence crucial for leadership roles? In this chapter, we will dig even further into this topic, examining how to improve the soft skills involved with emotional intelligence.

The Importance of Emotional Intelligence in the Workplace

80% of skills that differentiate top performers in the workplace are in the domain of emotional intelligence (IHHP, 2022). Out of thirty-three workplace skills, EQ was ranked number one in importance (Roy, 2022). 90% of top performers in the workplace have above-average EQ (Roy, 2022).

Without a doubt, your skills and intelligence may get you a job, but your EQ is what will help you retain it. Indeed, emotional intelligence is 58% of your job performance, regardless of your industry (Roy, 2022). If you are still not convinced, statistics show that your annual salary increases by $1,300 for every point increase in EQ. Overall, emotionally intelligent people also earn $29,000 more on average than their counterparts.

Emotional intelligence is your key tool for succeeding in the world, regardless of your industry or position. EQ isn't only essential for the workplace. Improving this skill will also help you with your personal relationships, whether that's a partner, children, or friends. And this is certainly appealing when you see how much you can reduce stress by being able to understand, monitor, predict, and handle others' feelings!

The Five Components of EQ

If you want to develop your emotional intelligence, you need to focus on these five components. Before discussing how to develop these components, you must understand what they mean. This section will give you a brief and factual look into what the five components are composed of.

Self-Awareness

Self-awareness can be boiled down to this basic definition: I understand what I feel and think, and I understand why I feel and think the way I do. Angela Ahrendts, Senior Vice President of Apple, said:

> "I have learned to listen and to hone my instincts, to be perceptive and to be receptive. To change. To constantly live in ambiguity. How else can leaders today look around the corner and warn others of what's coming? Only when you follow your instincts and continually renew your mind can your possibilities become realities."

Notice that she says she has learned to listen to herself. Self-awareness cannot be achieved unless you know who you are. Who we are is contained in our brains: how we think and feel. Once we understand these two things, we understand ourselves and develop self-awareness.

Self-Regulation

After self-awareness comes self-regulation. Self-awareness says, "I know why I feel angry." Self-regulation says, "Although I feel angry, it is not the best idea to react out of my anger by shouting at my employees. I will try to be calm at the moment and wait until I can go for a run to let off some steam."

Self-regulation also involves calming and comforting yourself when you feel negative emotions. So, if a person speaks to you rudely, although you might feel disrespected, you can say to yourself this person's actions are not reflective of your worth, and you do not need to respond rudely to prove a point. As a result, you're able to respond calmly and with respect. Without self-regulation, you might respond rudely, causing negative ramifications for your position as a leader, whereas if you respond calmly and respectfully, this will have positive ramifications for your position as a leader.

Self-regulation lets you stay in control of your emotions, meaning that you rarely act irrationally out of uncomfortable or negative emotions. When people project negative emotions onto others, verbally attack others, or make impulsive, emotional decisions, they are reacting out of their own negative or uncomfortable emotions. Self-regulation prevents impulsive reactions by holding yourself accountable when things go wrong rather than projecting your feelings onto others. Leaders who self-regulate quickly earn the respect of the people around them.

Empathy
Empathy refers to viewing a situation from another's perspective, even if the opinions differ from your own. You strive to understand other people's emotions and conditions that may have affected the current circumstances.

Motivation
Motivation is the desire and optimism to want to do something or act a certain way. You can be motivated to work hard, to be a reliable leader, and so on. Motivation is what causes us to act to make our desires and dreams come true.

Social Skills

Social skills are the skills that help us to verbally and non-verbally communicate with others. When you have good social skills, you can easily and effectively communicate with others, building positive relationships and forging connections with others. If you have bad social skills, you may find it difficult to build positive and strong relationships with others.

How to Build Your Emotional Intelligence

You can build your emotional intelligence by working on the five components:

Self-Awareness

A journal is a great way to help you improve your self-awareness. It allows you to write down your thoughts and feelings, especially those you have when particularly stressful or exciting events are happening. By reading through your journal, you can connect what you think and feel to how you react. For instance, you may notice a habit of reacting with extreme sadness when a team member leaves. Once you make this connection, you may dig deeper to figure out what about this is a trigger for you. Perhaps you moved schools a lot in childhood, causing you to react with excessive sadness when someone leaves you, no matter the reason. By examining your emotions and connecting them to past experiences, you will slowly build your self-awareness.

Self-Regulation

Learning your values as a person is the best way to learn self-regulation. When you do not compromise on your values, you are able to respond from these principles. Consequently, when you have to make ethical or moral decisions, you do not act out of your emotions but rather on more solid values.

Another way to improve self-regulation is to practice being calm. Meditative breaks with deep breathing practices and regular journaling are great methods to begin with. If you're angry or upset, take a moment to vent to a trusted friend (or therapist) if you need to release that initial frustration. Don't let it build up. Exercise and other active hobbies allow you to focus on positive actions that calm your mind and distract you from stress.

Empathy

You can improve your empathy by paying attention to people's body language and verbal communication. If their body language reflects sadness, you can analyze how they must feel and try to put yourself in their position. Think about how you would feel if you were in this person's position and plan your response from their point of view. In essence, respond to the person how you would hope someone else would respond to you if you were feeling the same negative emotions. Listen carefully to their concerns. Let them know how much they mean to you or how much you appreciate their work. Explore solutions that can help resolve their problems.

Motivation

If you want to develop motivation and the ability to consistently put hard work into reaching your goals, you need to spend time reflecting on why your goals matter to you. Reflect and remember why you love your career and why you chose leadership. US Congresswoman Cory Bush put it best when she described what exactly motivated her to chase after leadership:

> *"I ran and I lost and I ran and I lost. I kept running because there was a mission behind it. It wasn't about me wanting to be somebody*

in Congress—I know some people have those aspirations—but, for me, it was more about the mission... I am who I am. I don't take off my activist hat to be able to legislate in Congress. And so that has been the guiding force this entire time."

You can see that her motivation was derived from her values and self-awareness. Likewise, she was optimistic that she would eventually win, even in the face of failure.

Social Skills

You can develop your social skills by developing your communication skills. Learn how to resolve conflict by being open to hearing the truth from your team members, positive or negative. Explore how to inspire others through praise and positive attention. Build your team's confidence by listening carefully to their needs and responding accordingly with a plan of action.

Chapter Summary

- Emotional intelligence gives you the ability to recognize, understand, and manage your own emotions, as well as recognize, understand, and influence the emotions of others.

- Transformational leadership (a popular style among female leaders) is linked to emotional intelligence; hence, women tend to make excellent leaders.

- Emotional intelligence makes up 58% of your job performance, regardless of your industry.

- The five components of emotional intelligence are

self-awareness, self-regulation, motivation, empathy, and social skills.

It's time for you to take all the skills you have learned from the previous chapters and use them to create new opportunities, regardless of gender, race, or any other potential bias. In the next chapter, you will learn what workplace diversity is and why it is crucial in your workplace.

Setting the Example for a Diverse Environment

"We cannot all succeed when half of us are held back."
Malala Yousafzai

Despite the advances that women have made in the workforce in the past few decades, there is still a long way still to go. The same applies to people of color in the US workforce today. Men are already twice as likely to be hired, regardless of the gender of the hiring manager. At the same time, 78% of the US workforce is white (Reiners, 2021). Even though the US is a diverse nation, these disparities in hiring practices and in the racial makeup of its workforce obviously have far-reaching consequences for anyone who is not white and male.

Ironically, when it comes to blind hiring, women are more likely to be hired than men (Reiners, 2021). Diversity is a concept that the US still struggles with and one that many companies grapple with themselves. As a transformational leader, or any other type of leadership you develop, it's important to set an example for a diverse environment. In this chapter, you will learn what workplace diversity is and why it is so crucial, not just for women but for people from different backgrounds, be it their race, ethnicity, religion, nationality, sexuality, or anything else. This chapter will cover ways to improve your workplace culture, increase diversity, and encourage team members to strive for the same thing. It will also cover how leaders can promote a growth mindset and professional development within their team.

As a leader, promoting diversity is one of the most powerful things you can do. Anyone who does not fit into the dominant white patriarchal, heterosexual culture in America will tell you that this makes life much more difficult for them. By setting an example of diversity, you turn your power into influence, and what's more, you make other people's lives better and more rewarding. Condoleezza Rice, former US Secretary of State, said:

> "Power is nothing unless you can turn it into influence. When people talk about management style, they're really talking about how someone uses power. I've been in positions where I had to be heavy-handed, and I've been in positions where I needed to bring people together and persuade them... But sometimes you have to make difficult decisions, and you have to make them stick."

Why Is Diversity in the Workplace So Crucial?

A diverse workplace gives you access to a greater talent pool, with each individual bringing their own set of skills, experience, and ideas. Not only that, your employees feel they can trust you better when they see you trying to improve diversity in the workplace. It shows that you are emotionally intelligent and that you have morals and values. This, in turn, improves employees' morale, thereby boosting workplace productivity. Indeed, diversity within the workplace has been proven by studies to have a positive impact on employee morale, making employees more motivated to work effectively and efficiently (Yip, 2020). Diversity in the workplace also increases productivity because employees feel happier and more valued.

Your customers and clients will typically react positively to diversity, too. With a more diverse workforce, you will be better able to understand the needs of clients from various backgrounds. This has the potential to increase your customer base and your customers' trust. This also is a positive experience for potential employees, making recruitment much easier for you. When candidates visit your workplace and see that you have a diverse group of workers, they feel that they would blend into the team much easier because there are already people in your workforce who share similar experiences with them. Likewise, a more diverse workplace reduces conflict within the team. For example, having just one woman and twelve men on your team can make the woman feel alienated. She may feel that the men do not understand or accept her struggles and perspective, causing her to speak less at work. This reduces her morale and her effectiveness and efficiency at work. The men may also unconsciously alienate her from the team because they feel more comfortable with each other, talking about things that they may be interested in and therefore excluding her.

You also improve your workplace's reputation among all stakeholders when you promote diversity. You give your business a more competitive edge over bigger firms, and you attract new clients who choose their business based on whether workplaces are socially inclusive and promote good workplace culture.

One of my favorite benefits of having a diverse team is that we find answers to solutions to problems quickly. People from all walks of life bring a multifaceted and well-rounded perspective, enabling you to reach solutions quicker than if you had less diversity on your team. The Harvard Business Review (Reynolds and Lewis, 2017) states that workplace teams "solve problems faster when they're more cognitively diverse."

The data also backs the benefits of diversity in the workplace. More than 75% of workers prefer a diverse workplace when searching for employment (Reiners, 2021). This coincides with the new generation, Gen Z, who are made up of 48% racial and ethnic minorities (Reiners, 2021). It is predicted that minorities will become the majority in the United States by 2044, so by promoting a diverse workplace now, you are staying ahead of the curve (Reiners, 2021).

There are immediate benefits, too. Diverse companies benefit from a higher cash flow, 2.3 times higher per employee than their homogenous counterparts (Reiners, 2021) and are 36% more likely to perform better. Additionally, when you adopt a diversity-focused management style, you increase your revenue by 19%. Statistics show that gender-diverse organizations have a 15% higher chance of beating industry median financial returns (Reiners, 2021). Lastly, 73% of companies that promote gender equality show higher productivity and profits (What to Become, 2022).

What Is Workplace Culture?

Like diversity, workplace culture impacts performance, productivity, communication, recruitment, engagement, and retention—all parts of your workplace that decide the success of your company. Culture comprises attitudes, beliefs, and behaviors that make up the work environment. A bad office culture will lead to a toxic workplace and, ultimately, failure. So, how do you create a culture in the workplace that allows diverse ideas with an emphasis on communication and collaboration?

Culture should be decided by the team rather than dictated by the boss. One way to promote this is to find ways to boost your employees' moods and concentration. Find ways to make employees happy by communicating with them respectfully and fostering relationships based on mutual respect and trust. When employees come to you with ideas and criticism, allow them to speak without silencing them and without negative repercussions. Open communication creates an environment where people feel heard, validated, respected, and trusted. This improves employee happiness and promotes a positive workplace culture.

You must also keep in mind that people admire transparency. Employees need to believe that there is transparency in every part of the workplace. Once they begin to suspect that there might be lying or coverups, employees are less likely to engage in workplace culture or to communicate openly. This toxicity permeates your workplace and creates a negative workplace culture.

If your employees are not happy, they will not feel valued, and they will not feel like they are part of a community. Without a sense of community, transparency, and happiness, employees are more likely to find somewhere else to work, reducing your employee retention. Once too many team members begin to leave, the workplace may feel even less like a community, causing others to leave as well. Continuously replacing workers is another way to lose your workplace community and team spirit, and you will lose your workplace culture altogether or be left with an always shifting culture that never fully materializes.

Happy employees provide the best quality work. If your workplace culture is negative, it makes your workers unhappy, reducing employee output and quality and decreasing your profits and your company's reputation.

One highly effective way to improve employee culture is to send out surveys that enable you to find out what workplace culture your employees seek and how you can provide this. Questions such as "Do you feel respected by your manager, your teammates, and your organization?" and "If there was one thing you could change about the organization, what would it be?" are great ways to figure out how to produce a culture that makes your team happy.

You can also iconize your organization's values by setting them out in printed form and handing them out to potential and new employees. This way, they can familiarize themselves with these values before beginning at your company. You can do the same with your organization's policies, such as dress codes, training, and performance management.

Establishing a Growth Mindset Within Your Team

With a fixed mindset, employees struggle with change and avoid challenges. They believe that their skills and talents are set firmly as they are. You want to avoid this and, instead, establish a growth mindset. A growth mindset is when people understand their ability to improve, learn from their mistakes, and know what it takes to stay motivated. Above all, a growth mindset allows us to see the potential in all people, regardless of their background.

Here are five steps to promoting a growth mindset in the workplace:

Tie Performance Evaluation to Learning, Not Output

Employees are more likely to adopt a growth mindset when you tie their evaluations to learning and not output. This is because output is quantitative, and performance evaluations are qualitative. In a performance evaluation, you can discuss the different skills that an employee might seek to gain through training, education, and so on. On the other hand, output is dependent simply on producing more profits.

Focusing on quantitative profits only pressures your employee to work harder without the motivation to want to do more or to work effectively or efficiently. On the other hand, improving qualitative skills and experience produces more output in the long term, while also producing an employee who is more well-rounded, more qualified, and more motivated to continue to grow, to the benefit of your workplace.

Successes and Failures Are Learning Opportunities

In many workplaces, failures are often punished harshly. Employees are scared to admit to failure because they fear being fired or placed on suspension. When employees feel that failures will be placed on their permanent records, they are also more likely to cover it up, leading to problems for the company. For example, employees who fear punishment will likely not tell you the truth. They will adopt a culture of silence that will only serve to hurt your organization.

As a leader, it is better to develop a workplace culture where failures are handled as a stepping stone toward learning and doing better next time. This way, employees are given the mental and physical space to use their failures as a learning opportunity. At the same time, successes should not only be celebrated as an organizational success but also as the employees' successes. Your employees will feel valued when you celebrate their achievements, motivating them to learn and do more.

Give Employees the Chance to Speak

Giving employees a chance to speak is highly important to building an inclusive environment that's safe for a multitude of backgrounds. This open conversation is also great for boosting employee morale and creating a positive workplace culture. People want to be heard, not just commanded. Allow your employees to contribute to the ideas and resolutions of the company.

Invest in Upskilling

It can be difficult for employees to find the money, time, and resources to invest in improving their skills. Many organizations also fear investing in upskilling because they fear that employees might use their new skills to find better-paying jobs. However, by investing in upskilling, you invest in your workforce. An employee with better skills will put these skills to good use in your workplace. You also don't need to worry about your employees moving to a new workplace if you appropriately compensate them for their time and effort in developing a new skill. Another way to retain your employees after upskilling is to provide leadership opportunities where they can put their new skills into good use.

Support One-On-One Learning and Cross-Domain Learning

When someone begins a new position at a company, it can be challenging to identify upward advancement opportunities. If a team member is interested in helping with different projects, cross-domain learning allows your employee to temporarily transfer to another team and expand their expertise. Productivity is significantly more effective when your team can identify what they are passionate about. This can also build a greater appreciation and more precise vision for the company's accomplishments when employees can better understand their coworkers' responsibilities. Providing one-on-one learning with an admirable peer or with you as a coach can also expand your employee's future goals within the company as they witness the possible opportunities and explore new areas.

Increasing Diversity in Your Team

Some of the best ways of increasing diversity in your team include:
- Making employees feel valued, regardless of their background
- Practicing empathetic leadership
- Providing opportunities for employees to upskill and to move into leadership positions
- Spending time identifying and eliminating any biases that you might have
- Collaborating with your team to create your workplace's culture, vision, and policies
- Celebrating cultural differences among your team members
- Listening to your employees and making them feel heard and validated
- Creating connections and real relationships with your

employees

- Ensuring your recruitment strategy is not biased

In order to create a world that has no female leaders, just leaders, we need to change the focus from "fixing men" and "fixing women" because every person has something valuable to offer. Instead, if we increase diversity, we can fix the numerous issues that arise from biases.

Chapter Summary

- As a leader, promoting diversity is one of the most powerful things you can do.

- A diverse workplace gives you access to a greater talent pool, better employee retention, and a better company reputation.

- Workplace culture comprises attitudes, beliefs, and behaviors that make up the workplace environment.

- A growth mindset is when people understand that they have the ability to improve, learn from mistakes, and know what it takes to stay motivated.

In the next chapter, you will learn how to take time for yourself and put your health first before caring for everything and everyone. This final chapter is dedicated to ensuring women have everything it takes to manage both a leadership role and personal responsibilities so they can enjoy life to the fullest.

8
Self-Care and the Imperative Balance

"Trying to do it all and expecting that it all can be done exactly right is a recipe for disappointment. Perfection is the enemy."
Sheryl Sandberg

We can have it all—the family and the career—and succeed in both. But to do this, we must be able to take time for ourselves and put our health first. Only this way will we have enough time and energy to care for everything and everyone.

If we don't put ourselves first, we will eventually lose everything we took so much sweat, blood, and tears to build. This was certainly the case with a close acquaintance who started a fantastic catering business and was an immediate success. Like many women, she wanted to help as much as possible, be a part of her community, and support her family. Unfortunately, she had not learned how to say no and when to enforce her boundaries. Her phone was incessantly vibrating, with many people calling for additional help or favors. On the weekends, her entire day was packed with managing orders and trying to appease crazy last-minute demands. She never had time for herself, and her lack of boundaries started to eat into her professional and personal life. Yet, she continued to spread herself thin, giving too much of herself without saying no. Eventually, she ended up in the hospital with a host of issues that could have been prevented had she taken care of herself better and learned to balance her priorities.

There is only so much a person can take before they burn out! Yes, I know famous leaders make it look like it's easy to juggle work and family. This often makes us feel bad when we are having a difficult time. We feel as though we are doing something wrong. Remember that there will always be challenges, regardless of who you are. When Reese Witherspoon was asked about how she managed the work/life balance, she said, "I'm just trying to hold on, trying to make it through."

You, too, can make it through if you believe in your job as a leader and remember that you are setting an example for your children, and other women coming behind you, that will inspire them and drive their own passion.

The Silent Killer of the Workforce

Both neuroscience and neurobiology prove that women make better decisions under stress (Agaragimova, 2022). For many of us, we are accustomed to a fair amount of it, and in some cases, it can help us. However, there is a shocking amount of research on workplace stress and its negative impacts. Workplace stress is related to 120,000 deaths and almost $190 billion in healthcare costs annually (Workplace Mental Health, 2022). It is a silent killer. Yes, we want to be good leaders, but this does not have to come at the cost of our health. Health is everything, so be sure to watch out for the causes and physical and psychological symptoms of stress. That way, you can keep an eye out, responding quickly and swiftly with self-care if you need to combat stress.

Physical Symptoms of Stress
- Sleeping difficulties, e.g. insomnia
- Headaches
- Fatigue
- Muscular tension
- Heart palpitations
- Skin disorders
- Gastrointestinal problems, e.g. diarrhea or constipation

Psychological Symptoms of Stress
- Anxiety
- Depression
- Pessimism
- Irritability
- Discouragement
- Feeling overwhelmed
- Being unable to concentrate or make decisions

Causes of Stress in the Workplace
- Over-supervision/micro-management
- Being harassed or discriminated against at work
- Inadequate pay

- Job insecurity
- Inadequate working environment
- Misaligned workplace culture/values
- Boring work
- Long hours
- Tight/unrealistic deadlines
- Heavy workload
- Changes within the organization
- Changes to duties
- Lack of opportunities for advancement and promotions
- Lack of autonomy
- Insufficient skills
- Lack of proper resources
- Lack of equipment
- Poor relationships and connections with colleagues or bosses
- Crisis/traumatic incidents, such as a death in the workplace

Self-Care for Leaders

It is important to mention here that self-care is not something that should only be practiced by women! It's not about just pampering yourself or taking a yoga class every now and then. Self-care is about prioritizing your physical, mental, and emotional needs. Taking care of yourself is a sign of respect and helps to reduce stress and burnout both in the home and the workplace.

Regular self-care keeps you happy, focused, content, and emotionally regulated as a leader. These are essential qualities and states of being that you must pursue to create and preserve a happier workplace and environment among your team. If you're not emotionally well-regulated, you are prone to take it out on your team due to high-stress levels reducing your cognitive abilities. High-stress levels will also reduce your decision-making capacities, which can cause severe problems for your organization and your team. Finally, a considerate leader models self-care for their employees, promoting a workplace culture of regular self-care and self-love.

Self-Care for Your Professional Life

By practicing self-care in the workplace, you become more self-aware and are more likely to set healthy workplace boundaries. Train yourself to take regular breaks at work, plan your daily schedule, and give yourself and others grace when expectations are not met. You are not solely defined by your position. Disconnect from being a leader on your days off.

Self-Care for Your Personal Life

To help you practice self-care in your personal life, here is a list of twenty-five ideas to inspire you to set aside time to focus on yourself:

1. Drink water regularly.

2. Spend time playing with animals.

3. Get plenty of sleep and enjoy quick naps.

4. Participate in a crafting workshop.

5. Learn to play a new instrument.

6. Start your day doing something that makes you happy.

7. Jot down five things that went well daily.

8. Explore fitness classes at your local community center.

9. Take breaks from technology and give your brain and eyes regular breaks.

10. Write down all your negative thoughts about yourself, then rip up the paper.

11. Plan your meals for the week.

12. Take a new, scenic route to work.

13. Visit a different town near you and explore the area.

14. Meditate regularly.

15. Participate in a museum/national park tour.

16. Enjoy your first-morning cup of tea or coffee.

17. Spend five minutes at the end of your day to decompress.

18. Start a garden.

19. Volunteer occasionally for movements you're passionate about.

20. Go shopping.

21. Practice good posture; stand and sit straight with confidence.

22. Visit a new restaurant and try a different meal than you're accustomed to.

23. Start your day with a healthy, delicious breakfast.

24. Practice saying "no" more (and mean it).

25. Go for a walk in nature.

Remember that you don't have to get it all right all at once. Do what you can and let the rest fall in place in their own time!

Chapter Summary

- We can have it all—the family and the career—and still succeed in both.

- We must make time for ourselves and put our own health first if we want to succeed in family and career.

- Stress is the silent killer, so practice regular self-care to lower your stress levels.

Final Words

> "The day will come when man will recognize woman as his peer, not only at the fireside, but in councils of the nation. Then, and not until then, will there be the perfect comradeship, the ideal union between the sexes that shall result in the highest development of the race."
> Susan B. Anthony

    As a woman, one thing I can say about working within a predominantly male field as an Aviation Structural Mechanic in the Navy is that a change in leadership style is more refreshing than we realize and give credit to. During my final year in service, I was the one that was sought after for training periods because I knew how to lead with a firm, nurturing mindset, instead of the typical hardcore, condescending one. You'd be amazed how many military men greatly cherish a leader who is simply patient and encouraging with their coaching, regardless of their gender. When a particular type of leadership surrounds us, it's tempting to try replicating it to blend in and be accepted. Don't do that! Stand out by being yourself. Explore the leadership styles listed in Chapter Two and experiment with what fits most naturally with who you are. There's a workplace out there that needs someone just like you, so pursue being the best version of yourself that you can be.

    Despite centuries of the world trying to put us down, women have continued to rise up. We have achieved so much in so little time despite the odds being stacked against us. You can place a woman in a leadership position and, with the right training, skills, and confidence in herself, she will excel. I certainly excelled in my position in the Navy. I am proud of myself for standing my ground and leaning into my leadership style, despite the pressure I initially felt to conform to more traditionally masculine leadership conventions. Even so, it is not really about what is masculine and feminine. Until recently, what is said to be masculine was deeply encoded, and men were not tolerated to veer from that. Today, I have seen a change in the many men who also lean into transformational leadership, or their own personal brand of leadership, simply because it works!

Everyone is their own individual. Men and women should not be categorized into having certain personality traits. However, science does highlight differences in gendered behavioral patterns. It's not the differences that bring about challenges in female leadership; it's the biases, traditions, expectations, and conventions that people expect us to follow simply because we are women. I am happy to see so many people moving away from this belief and choosing to be their true selves, whether in their personal life or in their work life and leadership style. A sixty-year-old white man could be aggressive in his leadership skills, but that's not to say he doesn't respect the role of women in his company, including women of color. A twenty-year-old woman may be more inclined to vote for a female politician because she is more used to seeing gender balance in school and college. She may also choose to run because she believes she can make great changes in her community by doing so!

Whether you are beginning or continuing your journey as a leader, I have organized this book specifically for you. You have learned the fourteen major leadership styles used by leaders in the world today. Likewise, you now have a blueprint for creating your own personal leadership style. You now know the practical steps to take to overcome fear and self-doubt in a world that deliberately creates self-doubt in you. To top it off, you're armed with the seven hard skills that any confident and successful leader must use as a tool for effective leadership. You know how to tap into your inner self and speak out, using your voice as both a weapon and a shield: to defend, protect, accomplish, and lead. As a leader, you now understand the importance of emotional intelligence and of creating a diverse work environment and are armed with the importance of self-care for recharging and being the best you can be at all times.

I want to give women the wings they need to fly and soar. Like Ruth Bader Ginsburg said:

> "People ask me, 'When will you be satisfied with the number of women on the court?' When there are nine. For most of the country's history, they were all white men."

Just like Supreme Court Justice Ruth Bader Ginsburg, I want to do my part to uplift women worldwide who want to be great leaders, too. Until the world is fair and half the leaders in business, government, religion, and even family life are leaders, our job as women is never over. As you continue to fight the good fight, remind yourself of the different hard and soft skills available to you and how you can use each to better your leadership. Continue to practice and improve your communication skills and emotional intelligence until you become a pro! While it's perfectly normal to be afraid of a leadership role, you have all the tools you need to succeed within the pages of this book! And even if you haven't gotten that leadership role yet, continue to use the information packed into this book to make your way to your dreams.

Wherever you are in your journey, I leave you with these wise words from the CEO of Walgreens, Rosalind Brewer:

"I think about: Have I been bringing enough people along? You can help a peer become a CEO... This is not a competition or a race. We're better when we move in herds. This is a time for leaders to really evaluate themselves and say, 'Have I really been the servant leader that I thought I was?'"

If you found *She's Meant to Lead* helpful and would like to support the Kyrabe Stories community, we'd greatly appreciate it if you'd take a few minutes to leave a quick, honest review. Not only do your reviews help authors, but there are so many other women who want to lead but don't feel like they are capable. Your review could be what inspires other women to take that all-important step! Remember, we need all the women we can get into leadership positions to continue our great fight!

Scan to Leave a Review

References

Acha, K. (2019, September 30). The PREP Framework: An Easy Way to Give Excellent Impromptu Speeches. Kenneth Acha Ministries.

Agaragimova, E. (2022, May 10). Women May Make Better Leaders Than Men, Science Shows: Feminine Leadership Qualities That Drive Success. Training Industry.

Alexander, K.L. (2022). Malala Yousafzia. National Women's History Museum.

Ariella, S. (2022. April 19). 25 Women in Leadership Statistics [2022]: Facts on the Gender Gap in Corporate and Political Leadership. Zippia.

AZ Quotes. (2022). Female Leaders Quotes. AZ Quotes.

Batchelder, C. (2022). What Is Strategic Leadership and How to be a Strategic Leader. Lifehack.

Bay Area Council. (2017, July 31). Addressing Gender Bias in Workplace Communications. Bay Area Council.

Better Health. (2022). Work-Related Stress. Better Health.

Bolotnyy, V. & Emmanuel, N. (2022, July 1). How Unpredictable Schedules Widen the Gender Pay Gap. HBR.

Brinn, J. (2014, June 17). Leadership Styles Part 1: Authoritarian Leadership. Michigan State University,

Catalyst. (2022, March 1). Women in Management. (Quick Take). Catalyst.

Cavanaugh, L.V. (2022). Our List of Top Women's Leadership Blogs. Progressive Women's Leadership.

Cherry, K. (2020, April 29). How a Transactional Leadership Style Works. Verywell Mind.

REFERENCES

Cherry, K. (2022, May 23). What Is Democratic Leadership? Verywell Mind.

Cottier, C. (2021, February 23). Queen Kubaba: The Tavern Keeper Who Became the First Female Ruler in History. Discover Magazine.

Croft, A. (2022, August 22). How to Build and Lead a Diverse Team and Why You Need It. Everhour.

Driven Woman. (2022). The 20 Best Women's Networks to Help You Achieve Your Goals. Driven Woman.

Edwards, V.V. (2022). Women in Leadership: 6 Strategies for Female Managers. Science of People.

Gavin, M. (2020, January 9). 7 Strategies for Improving Your Management Skills. Harvard Business School.

Gilbert, M. (2017, November 22). Self-Doubt Is Sabotaging your Leadership. Here's How to Break the Cycle and Lead with Confidence. Inc Africa.

Griffin, T. (2020, May 13). 6 Best Ways Leaders Can Boost Their Analytical Skills. Business 2 Community.

HPPY. (2022). How to Develop Leadership Skills in HR. HPPY.

HR Future. (2022, August 9). Women in Leadership: How to Overcome Anxiety. HR Future.

IHHP. (2022). The Meaning of Emotional Intelligence. IHHP.

Indeed. (2020, April 17). Affiliative Leadership: Definition. Benefits and Tips. Indeed.

Instagantt. (2022). A Guide on Top 10 Skills for Effective Communication (Updated October 2022).

LaMantia. B. & Ma, J. (2022, February 2). 25 Famous Female Leaders on Power. The Cut.

Linberg, C. (2022). Pacesetting Leadership - What Is It? Pros/Cons? Examples? Leadership Ahoy.

LR Success. (2022, April 27). Strategic Leadership: Pros and Cons. LR Success.

Lucas, S. (2021, September 27). Visionary Leadership. The Balance Money.

Mayer J. D., Salovey P. (1997). What Is Emotional Intelligence? In Salovey P., Sluyter D. (Eds.), *Emotional development and emotional intelligence: Implications for educators* (pp. 3-31). New York: Basic Books.

Meier, K.S. (2018, July 1). Gender Barriers to Communication. Chron.

Meshkat, M., & Nejati, R. (2017). Does Emotional Intelligence Depend on Gender? A Study on Undergraduate English Majors of Three Iranian Universities. *SAGE Open, 7*(3).

Michals, D. (2015). Amelia Earhart. National Women's History Museum.

Michals, D. (2015). Sojourner Truth. National Women's History Museum.

Mind Tools. (2022). Emotional Intelligence in Leadership. Mind Tools.

National Park Service. (2022). Sojourner Truth: Ain't I a Woman? NPS.

Noteworthy Nonsense. (2022). Maya Angelou: How You Made Them Feel. Noteworthy Nonsense.

Project Practical. (2022). Emergent Leadership Explained with Examples. (Project Practical).

Purdue University Global. (2020, April 17). What Is Servant Leadership? Purdue University Global.

Rai, T. (2022). How to Improve your Computer Skills to Get Ahead in Your Career. Lifehack.

Roy, B.D. (2022, October 12). Understanding and Utilizing Emotional Intelligence in the Workplace. Vantage Circle.

Quotes Gram. (2022). Importance of Communication Quotes. Quotes Gram.

Reiners, B. (2021, October 21). 57 Diversity in the Workplace Statistics You Should Know. Built In.

Ramboll. (2022, March 7). Spotlight on Gender Bias. Ramboll.

Reynolds, A. & Lewis, D. (2017, March 30). Teams Solve Problems Faster When They're More Cognitively Diverse. Harvard Business Review.

Schawbel. D. (2022, February 21). 6 Reasons Why Leaders Should Prioritize Self-Care. Linked In.

Shannon-Karasik, C. (2018, November 13). 25 Ways You Can Practice Self-Care Every Single Day. Women's Health Mag.

Suder, R. (2022). What Are Hard Skills? Top Resume.

Sutton, J. (2021, April 11). What Is the Coaching Leadership Style? Positive Psychology.

The University of Texas. (2022). How Much of Communication is Nonverbal? The University of Texas.

WE Forum. (2020, April 2). Why Coronavirus Could Reverse Progress on Closing the Gender Pay Gap. WE Forum.

Workplace. (2022). What Is Workplace Culture: An In-Depth Look. Workplace.

UN Women. (2022). Facts and Figures: Women's Leadership and Political Participation. UN Women.

Unconscious Bias Project. (2022). What Is Unconscious Bias? Unconscious Bias Project.

What To Become. (2022, August 3). The Importance of Diversity in the Workplace - 20 Key Statistics. What To Become.

Workplace Mental Health. (2022). Workplace Stress. Workplace Mental Health.

Yip, M. (2020, July 2). 12 Reasons Why Diversity is Important in the Workplace. Hive Life.

Acknowledgements

Kyrabe Stories was founded by Kyndall Bennett, a veteran passionate about education and leadership. Her experiences in the US Navy have given her a deep insight into women's struggles in a male-dominated workforce. Through her career exploration journey into the eLearning industry, she realized a need for a safe, educational place to provide professional development resources and relatable stories to those who desired a change in their lives but weren't sure where to begin.

z

With such an overwhelming response to Kyrabe Stories, Kyndall collaborated with the Publishing Services research team along with the writing and editing professionals, Hanah Johnson and Aimee Jodoin, to construct this book. Kyndall is striving to help more women improve their personal and professional development, unleash their confidence, and advance the necessary skills they need for leadership.

To explore additional resources, you can visit the Kyrabe Stories blog at KyrabeStories.com. You can also connect with Kyndall Bennett on LinkedIn at LinkedIn.com/in/KyndallBennett

Follow Kyrabe Stories on social media:
- Twitter: @KyrabeStories
- Facebook: @KyrabeStories

ACKNOWLEDGEMENTS

- TikTok: @KyrabeStories
- Instagram: @KyrabeStories

Printed in Great Britain
by Amazon